Palgrave Studies in African Leadership

Series Editors
Faith Ngunjiri, Global Leadership Development LLC, Windham, NH, USA
Nceku Nyathi, Royal Holloway University of London, Egham, UK

Almost every continent has solid representation in the field of leadership studies except for Africa, despite its rapid growth. A groundbreaking series, Palgrave Studies in African Leadership fills a gap in the production of knowledge and scholarly publishing on Africa and provides a much needed outlet for the works of scholars interested in African leadership studies around the world. Where many studies of leadership in Africa focus solely on one country or region, this series looks to address leadership in each of the different regions and countries of the continent. This comes at a time when business and academic discourse have begun to focus on the emerging markets across Africa. The wide-ranging scholarly perspectives offered in this series allow for greater understanding of the foundation of African leadership and its implications for the future. Topics and contributors will come from various backgrounds to fully explore African leadership and the implications for business, including scholars from business and management, history, political science, gender studies, sociology, religious studies, and African studies. The series will analyze a variety of topics including African political leadership, women's leadership, religious leadership, servant leadership, specific regions, specific countries, specific gender categories, specific business entities in Africa, and more.

Alette Vonk · Vasco Freitas Silva

Cultural Confluence in Organizational Change

A Portuguese Venture in Angola

palgrave
macmillan

Alette Vonk
Faculty of Humanities
Leiden University
Leiden, The Netherlands

Vasco Freitas Silva
Fafe, Portugal

ISSN 2945-6673 ISSN 2945-6681 (electronic)
Palgrave Studies in African Leadership
ISBN 978-3-031-45402-8 ISBN 978-3-031-45403-5 (eBook)
https://doi.org/10.1007/978-3-031-45403-5

This Palgrave Macmillan imprint is published by the registered company Springer Nature Switzerland AG
The registered company address is: Gewerbestrasse 11, 6330 Cham, Switzerland

Paper in this product is recyclable.

Together we will rise

Vasco Freitas Silva

Foreword

When I was asked to check the theory part, I accepted with a sense of duty. Soon, I found myself reading with a sense of wonder. I read all of it.

This book is alive. It's a duet. First and foremost, it's the story of a strike in a European-led, African company, told by the manager. At the same time, this book reflects on what happens, through a consultant's voice. It uses theory in the best possible way, to make sense of the episode so that readers can make the link to their own predicaments.

The book confirms Kurt Lewin's quip that nothing is more practical than a good theory. The main theory brought to life here is Hofstede's theory on culture. I mean the well-validated national culture dimensions, not the tentative work on organizational culture. Another theory used is Toyota's principle of "Genchi Genbutsu": when stuck, go see for yourself.

The case is Angolan. It unpacks the fact known across sub-Saharan Africa but rarely discussed, that there are two ways to do everything: one traditional, and one Western. In foreign-led multinationals, this dichotomy can create a communication gap. In the case company, a working solution is found that combines the two. It gave ears to the boss, and a voice to the frontline workers. This is just one company in a vast continent—but I believe that this kind of new synthesis can help get Africa out of its post-colonial trauma. The authors call it "confluence": the merging of two streams.

The country manager, Silva, is Portuguese. By European standards this society is closer to African values than most, and belonging is an important theme. For a country manager from other non-African countries to be as honestly involved, and as considerate, as Silva, will be challenging but potentially very rewarding. African managers too can try whether the shoe fits them. In fact, anyone in a leadership role in an international organization can benefit from the book's story. Business students not yet in such a leadership role should read it too and discuss it in class.

Together we will rise!

Ede, The Netherlands
August 2023

Gert Jan Hofstede

Acknowledgements

Not surprisingly, it is not possible nor desirable to write a book in a vacuum. There are various persons involved and we're very grateful for their support in many ways. We would like to thank Isabel Parenthoen and Jan Vincent Meertens for reading and commenting on an earlier version of the book and providing feedback that made us reflect and improve. This is also true for the reviewers from Palgrave Macmillan, their feedback was invaluable. We are grateful for the positive feedback of and the foreword by Prof. G.J. Hofstede. We thank Dr. Michael Eze for the very valuable conversations we had about the content of this book and Dr. Eva Jordans for providing us with valuable contacts. Prof. Catia Antunes was very helpful in pointing out new bodies of literature, and this is true for Bontle Marumoloa and Dr. Louise Müller as well, the last one always lending a listening ear on top.

Furthermore, we would like to express our heartfelt appreciation to the Angolan business owners and others, namely Paulino Neto, João Jardim, Lucas Bona, and Maria Miguel, for the inspiring insights regarding the Angolan culture. Also, we want to give a special thanks to the Rotary Club of Luanda Sul members for all the support and kindness. Last but not least, we would like to express our deep gratitude to the company and all the people who worked with Silva, both in Portugal and in Angola. Together we have chosen not to mention any names in this book, in order to protect the privacy of all people involved, but we do owe all of them a huge thank you for the incredible times spent together.

Competing Interests

The authors of this book have received no grants, nor was it written in company time. It was produced in evenings and weekends, and during breaks and vacations from other work-related activities and assignments. Yet, it is clear that both authors have an interest in the content of the book. At the time, Silva was the Country Director, and he clearly had a keen interest to make his subsidiary into a success, which is why he geared his organization on the transformative journey that is described. The positive results do improve his credibility as a manager for future positions as well. Vonk is a lecturer at Leiden University, but the greater part of the week, she's an independent entrepreneur, providing training and process consultancy on intercultural management. Therefore, she is convinced of but also has an interest in spreading stories that show the importance of cultural knowledge and competency in design and strategic decision making within organizations. On top, Silva and Vonk have launched the website www.spacesofconfluence.com together, to explain the approach and to create a space and invite other managers, entrepreneurs, and scholars to share more stories on cultural confluence and spread the word further.

Ethical Approval

For reasons of privacy, the authors have decided not to provide any names of the people featuring in this story. They have received written consent of the persons who were quoted literally.

Contents

About the Authors

Alette Vonk holds an M.Sc. Development Sociology from the University of Leiden in the Netherlands. She worked in the development business in West Africa for 10 years, in gender, good governance, and organizational development (Benin and in Ghana). Since 2010 she is an independent consultant (De Vonk advies en diversiteit) on intercultural management and organizational change, having clients among private companies, development NGO's and governmental entities. Finally, she's a lecturer Intercultural Management at the University of Leiden. She's written articles on doing business in Kenya on the Cube In Platform; written articles for the Xpat Journal, Newsletter Jobnet Africa, and on LinkedIn. Publications also include:

- OD Approaches and other cultures (OD Practitioner, vol 48, nr. 3, 2016).
- Interactieve benaderingen langs de culturele meetlat (M&O, jrg. 71, nr. 1, 2017).
- Vonk, A., Lanzer, F., Wijnands, J., Nunes Pereira de Souza, J. (2020). See what the Dutch Say, published independently: Amazon.

https://www.devonkadvies.nl; www.cultural-insights.nl; http://spacesofconfluence.com; https://www.linkedin.com/in/alettevonk/.

Vasco Freitas Silva graduated in Chemical Engineering at the Porto University, in 2001, with one of the best final classifications in his course (16 out of 20). After being granted with a scholarship grant from the Portuguese Government, he attended and accomplished his Ph.D. in Chemical Engineering, doing science research in two German research institutes, GKSS and German Aerospace Centre (DLR). After finishing his Ph.D. and publishing 13 science articles in international reviews, 3 science articles in Portuguese reviews and one book chapter, he started his management career journey with several roles, such as, R&D manager, Sales Manager, Agency Manager, Country Manager and, finally, Board Member. In 2010, he embraces an almost 7 years business mission in Angola, sub-Saharan Africa, starting a Engineering company agency from a multinational Portuguese company present in several countries (Brazil, Spain, Mozambique). During his Africa mission, he attended several executive training programmes at the Harvard Business School, having the Alumnus status of this United States University. At the moment, he has the role of executive board member of Strong Charon SA, a leading security company in Portugal. https://www.linkedin.com/in/vssilva/.

List of Figures

List of Tables

CHAPTER 1

Introduction

Abstract The introduction starts with the conversation between the Country Director Silva of a Portuguese subsidiary in Angola, and his boss in Portugal. Silva has been shocked by a wild strike of his front-line workers. It is the start of a transformative journey for him and his organization. The introduction provides some background to the passage from Silva to Angola and his first years of executing the 'best management practices'. Suddenly he realizes that it isn't sufficient. The aim of the book is to tell the story of the novel management approach Silva took, creating a culturally hybrid organization and making use of both Portuguese and Angolan, indigenous forms of leadership. The book is meant for scientists, who ask for such descriptive case studies, as well as business leaders, managers, and facilitators, who can be inspired to follow this example. The content of the book is described, and some background is provided about the authors, since this book is a joined production of Silva (as a personal testimony) and Vonk, an intercultural lecturer and consultant, who puts the whole story into perspective.

Keywords Angola · Best management practices · Risk management · Wild strike · Frontline workers · Hybrid organization · Indigenous leadership

A. Vonk and V. F. Silva, *Cultural Confluence in Organizational Change*, Palgrave Studies in African Leadership,
https://doi.org/10.1007/978-3-031-45403-5_1

Help! None of Our Local Employees Came to Work! Our Client Will Kill Us...

Saturday, 14 pm, Fafe, Portugal

Silva: *Boss, I just received a call from Angola stating that none of the employees has turned up to work on our major project. The client is already threatening with the application of huge contract penalties!*

Boss: *What happened?*

Silva: *The operations manager says that the frontline employees were complaining regarding the extra-hour payments and our foreman didn't seem to have given the right importance to the issue.*

Boss: *Ok! Solve it and then give me feedback...*

"Help! What's happening?! Why are our employees behaving this way? I don't understand!" These sentences capture the sentiment echoed so frequently by leaders acting in different cultural environments. Leaders, whether managers of multinational companies, heads of non-governmental organizations or non-profits, may find themselves suddenly slapped in the face with surprises due to cultural differences, which are so often unperceived, unacknowledged or neglected.[1] Unfortunately it is very common that the lack of good cultural knowledge leads to multinational company's losses, leader's career failure, missed opportunities and premature termination of contracts, joint ventures, and partnerships. Cultural differences actually form a strategic risk that calls for serious risk management.

The above situation is captured from a case which will be described, and which forms the backbone of this book. It is Silva, a Portuguese Country Manager, talking to his boss in Portugal. Silva has developed a subsidiary, a business in Angola, sub-Saharan Africa. Together with his management team in Angola, he had followed all the 'best management practices' according to his previous experience at the company Head Quarters (HQ). Being part of a Portuguese multinational company (MNC), starting off with its first business in Angola, they had performed a

[1] Ball et al. (2004).

study into the local business environment. From the start they had established a hiring procedure with clear criteria for both local employees and expats; they had studied books and articles about local culture; attended seminars and workshops regarding the Angolan business environment; and they had regular talks with expats that had lived and worked in Angola.

In fact, due to all this preparation and hard work, and after some years of business development, with almost a continuous 100% annual revenue growth in the Angolan industrial refrigeration market, the company started to have a good set of excellent clients and a stable operations team of almost 80 employees, mainly from Angola. At the time, it seemed that they were doing everything right. They had a good portfolio of successful projects; a well-established hierarchical structure; financial health and strong HR policies (performance evaluation, recruitment criteria, intensive technical training programme, etc.). But despite being good followers and executers of these best practices, they had no idea that they were dangerously walking at the edge of failure, and they experienced a painful event regarding their frontline workers, that almost killed their company.

Silva: One Saturday I was on vacation in my hometown, Fafe in Portugal, and I received an urgent international phone call from our operations manager. He sounded very disturbed, saying that all the frontline employees, constructing a major refrigeration facility on-site, some 3 to 4 kilometres from the office in Luanda, had not shown up for work. This assignment was the biggest granted to us so far (almost 1 million USD) and was far from being completed. Work continued during the weekends, as it often did, and usually employees were happy to work these hours, due to the financial measures for extra-time. Desperately, we tried to call each one of our employees by phone. Without success. They were totally unreachable. All of them.

The HR manager explained over the phone that the frontline employees had been complaining regarding the extra-hour payments and an assistant had gone to the site on Friday to settle the issue. The manager thought it had been dealt with, but he would immediately start recalculating and looking further into the issue. The next day, Sunday, all the frontline employees remained unreachable, and the problem became more and more severe. We were hopeless! Our client was indeed threatening with the application of contract penalties, and this could result in huge losses for our company, even bankruptcy.

Monday came and all the employees turned up at the construction site, as if nothing had happened. They were called to the office and finally the extra-time issue was clarified. It turned out that there had indeed been a measurement problem and the employees were justified in their complaint. Besides, we came to understand that the frontline workers had been upset by the way they had been spoken to, telling them to stop complaining and go back to work.

After the problem had become clear and solved, the client appeased and the dust settled, I started to notice a structural issue concerning our very limited information flow from the frontline workers to the management team (bottom-up). The motivations, considerations, thoughts, and decisions of our employees appeared like a black box to me, our cultural knowledge to predict their behaviour seemed suddenly very limited.

Slowly we realized that the management and leadership practices emanated from my previous management experience were planned as 'one size fits all,' while many of them would probably require some adaptation. Literature told us that without cultural context tailoring in strange markets, practices have a tendency to be either rejected or adopted only ceremonially, thus not achieving the desired results.[2] *Something was wrong and we had to reinvent our cross-cultural leadership practices urgently, to prevent further "ignorance tax" payment.*[3] *If not, it seemed our company reputation could be ruined in a few days, while it had taken years to build. It was clear: we had some serious work to do.*

After this traumatic event, diving into books and doing some serious soul searching, we decided to perform a deep study of the Angolan culture and to develop an innovative, culture sensitive management approach. Local, Angolan ideas and practices about leadership, organization, and internal communication were introduced and penetrated deeply into the existing best practices from our Portuguese HQ and it led to a somewhat culturally hybrid organization, with western, Portuguese, and also some Angolan features.

[2] Bartlet and Ghoshal (1989).

[3] Hamel (2007, p. 204).

The Aim of the Book

The aim of this book is to tell a story. First and foremost, the book is based on this case study, describing the successful implementation of a culture specific transformative process. It is quite rare to find such a strategically planned effort of a foreign MNC to take African local culture into account and to invite local notions about leadership and organization this far into its structures. On top, it took courage of the relatively young Angolan employees, to use these heavily loaded cultural concepts in a creative manner, even to embody and enact them. All in all, it is a story that deserves to be told.

Taking the story as the point of departure, most chapters of this book follow the line of action, as it was executed in practice by Silva. A large part of the book reads like a management road movie, if you will, inviting the reader to embark on the journey with him, a Portuguese Country Director in an Angolan context.

The story-aspect is emphasized because there is not one 'correct' answer for leadership and management challenges on this huge and enormously varied continent. It is exactly this form of experimentation and such descriptive examples that many African scholars and management scientists have called for, in order to rebuild theories and models.[4] The book, in that sense, may be called a monography.

One of the target groups of the book, therefore, is made up of these scientists: the sociologist, anthropologist, social economist, historian, or philosopher. The story is embedded in an historical and theoretical framework, which will be explained in part I, where the stage is being set. Subsequently, while Silva tells his story (*in italics*) and the tale unfolds, we tap in and out of the various scientific resources and management literature from different backgrounds (African, Western, and Japanese). The main course of reasoning is that cultures are not essentialist, rigid entities, with little room for change. Rather, the case study reveals that, while some basic values may have a great impact on behaviour, there is a large space for flexibility and in fact, in the words of Eze and Van der Wal, for multi-layered identities and the 'confluence,' or interweaving, of cultures.[5] The question posed is how the new key fits the new lock.

[4] Iguisi (2014, p. 74), Iwowo (2015), Gyekye (1997, 2004), Bhengu (2011), Lessem and Nussbaum (1996), Nkomo (2011, p. 379), and Dia (1996).

[5] Eze and Van der Wal (2020, p. 204).

The target group that is at least as important is the practitioner: business leaders, change agents, and managers of multinational organizations (whether profit or not-for-profit). The book provides a grand outline of a cultural transformative process of a European organization on the African continent, and they can grasp how scientific knowledge can provide very useful insights for their strategies. It showcases that setting up business (in general but specifically in a strange context) doesn't call for 'quick fits' but rather might call for a willingness to take the extra mile on a complicated, yet fascinating road with several curves and loopholes. All in all, we hope that this narrative will be an inspiring guide for both African and international (business) leaders and facilitators to research, plan, and build novel management approaches based on a combination of values and concepts.

The Content of the Book

The book is divided into four parts. The first part will be setting the stage for the story to unfold. It starts with a description of the first steps Silva took just after the wild strike. He dived back into his management books and read them with new eyes, while also doing some serious soul searching to raise the cultural awareness of himself and his management team. At the end of the chapter, Silva formulates the ultimate goal of the organizational change journey he was about to start. The second chapter of part I recounts the larger context in which this narrative is taking place. The daunting challenge in Africa below the Sahara to deal with its disruptive history will be briefly outlined; the search for indigenous forms of leadership, management, and organization and the efforts to reconcile a mosaic of cultural logic and institutions.

In part II the research into culture and intercultural management takes place. The research is divided into two areas of cultural study: an etic (from the outside) and an emic (from the inside) approach. The etic research, in Chapter 4, gives us a chance to compare cultures and is executed through the cultural dimensions of Hofstede.[6] After a necessary discussion of the pros and cons of this model, the different basic values of Angola, Portugal, and the USA (where most management literature originates) are compared and used to throw light on the situation

[6] Hofstede et al. (2010).

leading up to the strike. It also provides Silva with clues as to how to proceed into the future. For the emic approach, in Chapter 5, an adaptation of Toyota innovation philosophy, named *Genchi Genbutsu*[7] is being applied. In English, this practice is usually translated as a directive to 'go and see for yourself.' For the company it involved formulating questions, interviewing employees, having open conversations with other local inhabitants and validation with local business leaders. Sound explanations and experiences are being described, about local wisdom, customs, values, and beliefs, which inspired management to develop a culture specific intervention. The chapter ends with the formulation of a small list of Angolan cultural elements that were found in the research, which would guide the change process.

Part III is the most practical part of the book. It describes the organizational change that was adopted. Using the elements of the research, the company was able to combine the best of both worlds. Chapter 6 provides the design: the set-up, expectations, organization, and formulation of mission, values, and activities of a new to form Culture Council, as an innovative organ within the company structure, enabling the involvement of frontline workers and bridging the gap with management. In Chapter 7 named 'Reaping the harvest,' the extensive results of one-and-half year of implementation of the Culture Council, frequently called the Soba Council, are reported. The adventurous road, with its structural results, interesting anecdotes and organized events is accounted for and the chapter ends with the evaluation that was executed.

Part IV is the conclusion and embodies one chapter: Chapter 8, with a wrap-up and taking some lessons and steps into the future. What does this case study tell us about the confluence of cultures, and the notions of modernism and contemporary tradition? Why is the Culture Council in this case study different from a Works Council? And what were the specific adaptations and performative (flexible) aspects of Angolan Soba leadership, on the one hand, and of Portuguese, foreign leadership, on the other? The chapter ends with some consequences for HR policy and with some meaningful and overall concluding remarks of Silva.

[7] Liker (2004).

About the Authors

This book is written in collaboration between Vasco Freitas Silva and Alette Vonk.

Silva is the Country Director of the firm. He is the initiator of the subsidiary, the creative mind behind the intercultural change process and he went through all the ups and downs on this bumpy road. He wrote a personal testimony of his organizational change process, which is found back in italics throughout this book.

Alette Vonk is a development sociologist, intercultural consultant, and university lecturer from the Netherlands. She has lived and worked in West Africa for ten years (Cameroon, Benin, and Ghana) and travelled several countries in Southern Africa. She has visited the company in Angola, visited some construction sites, had qualitative interviews with several employees, sat in on a Council meeting, and had never-ending conversations with Silva. She used all this input, together with relevant literature and analysis, to put the whole case story into perspective and draw some conclusions.

References

Ball, D. A., McCulloch, Jr., W.H., Frantz, P. L., Geringer, J. M., & Minor, M. S. (2004). *International business: The challenges of global competition* (9th ed.). McGrawHill Irwin.

Bartlett, C. A., & Ghoshal, S. (1989). *Managing across boarders: The transnational solution*. Harvard Business School Press.

Bhengu, M. J. (2011). *African economic humanism: The rise of an African economic philosophy*. Gowing Publishing Limited.

Dia, M. (1996). *Africa's management in the 1990's and beyond: Reconciling indigenous and transplanted institutions*. The International Bank for Reconstruction and Development, The World Bank.

Eze, M. O., & Van der Wal, K. (2020). Beyond sovereign reason: Issues and contestations in contemporary African identity. *Journal of Common Market Studies, 58*(1), 189–205.

Gyekye, K. (1997). *Tradition and modernity: Philosophical reflections on the African experience*. Oxford University Press.

Gyekye, K. (2004). *The unexamined life: Philosophy and the African experience*. Sankofa Publishing Company.

Hamel, G. (2007). *The future of management*. Harvard Business School Press.

Hofstede, G., Hofstede, G. J., & Minkov, M. (2010). *Cultures and organizations: Software of the mind*. McGraw-Hill.

Iguisi, O. (2014). African values for the practice of HRM. *Beykent University Journal of Social Sciences, 7*(1), 56–77.

Iwowo, V. (2015). Leadership in Africa: Rethinking development. *Personnel Review, 44*(3), 408–429.

Liker, K. J. (2004). *The Toyota way: 14 management principles from the world's greatest manufacturer*. McGraw-Hill.

Lessem, R., & Nussbaum, B. (1996). *Sawubona Africa: Embracing four worlds in South African management*. Zebra Press.

Nkomo, S. M. (2011). A postcolonial and anti-colonial reading of 'African' leadership and management in organization studies: Tensions, contradictions and possibilities. *Organization, 18*(3), 365–386.

PART I

Setting the Stage

After starting up the company, experiencing growth and success, it was now time to stand still. Such is the time for a managing director to feel the loneliness of his job and the weight of his responsibility.

There is no story that takes place in a vacuum. Any story is situated within a larger context, and it was time for Vasco to study his surroundings far better for a moment. In this case, there is both a context of ideas about globalization, management, business and organization, and a geographical, historical context of the realities in which people live. This multi-layered stage will be set in this part I, which is made up of two chapters. In Chapter 2, the stage is set at company level. The tale starts with the Country Director Silva setting up business in Angola and, after the dust of the employees' strike had settled, his first steps in grappling with the recent events. Searching within his management literature, he posed himself and his surroundings some pertinent questions to raise his own awareness and that of the management team. He ended up looking at his company with new eyes. Suddenly the curtains had a different colour then he had seen so far, so to speak. The chapter ends with his preliminary conclusion and with the ultimate goal he set for his company, as it embarks on a transformative journey.

Before this journey gains further momentum, it is necessary to set the stage in a much wider African context and within a theoretical framework. Chapter 3 zooms out to African history and the sociocultural environment of today. This chapter deals with the challenges of African institutionalization, with African management philosophy and the search for reconciliation between indigenous and foreign systems of organization and leadership on the continent. Taking the story of Silva as a case study, the theoretical question posed is what could be said in the end about the confluence of cultures and the creative adaptation from both the Angolan and the Portuguese side.

CHAPTER 2

Globalization, 'Best' Management Practices, and Cultural Awareness

Abstract The Country Director Silva dives into his management books and reads them with new eyes, while doing some serious soul searching to raise the cultural awareness of himself and his management team. Ghemawat developed the CAGE framework, describing four areas of distance and subsequent risk for multinational companies, and Silva understands his subsidiary has hit the C of Cultural distance. Deeper layers of culture are situated within the unconscious minds, creating a blind spot for many managers and Silva recognizes this to be true for his predominantly Portuguese management team. Another model is the EPG model of Perlmutter, the global strategic profiles of multinationals: ethnocentric, polycentric, and geocentric profiles. Silva notices that his 'best' management practices emanate from HQ, are not as culture neutral as he thought and that his present structures are not capable to create sufficient internal information flow. He realizes he needs to become more geocentric. He then formulates the ultimate goal: to research culture much further and develop a culture-specific intervention. The objective is to embark on a transformative change process that will be vested in simple, genuine, and logical local concepts.

Keywords Cultural distance · Layers of culture · Geocentric · Ethnocentric · Transformative change · Internal information flow

A. Vonk and V. F. Silva, *Cultural Confluence in Organizational Change*, Palgrave Studies in African Leadership,
https://doi.org/10.1007/978-3-031-45403-5_2

Setting Up Business in Far-Away Markets

Globalization is the process through which an increasingly free flow of ideas, people, goods, services, and capital leads to the integration of economies and societies.[1] In the years after the recession of 2007–2009, the appetite for investment in emerging markets, like several African countries, sharpened considerably in Latin Europe. There was a recession at home and labourers, companies, and entrepreneurs were attracted by the economic growth that had taken place in these markets in the years prior to the recession and the vast potential of a largely untapped market.[2] "According to estimations from the OECD (2011, p. 52), Angola was for a couple of years, one of the fastest growing economies in the world, and GDP growth rates were 20,6% in 2005, 18,6% in 2006 and as much as 27% in 2007."[3] These can be called the "golden years" in Angola "and during these years the inflow of Portuguese migrants grew rapidly."[4]

The Portuguese corporation, where I worked, was one of many multinational corporations with mature businesses, looking for growth opportunities in far-away markets, and the venture, I set up as a Country Director in Angola, was the first African adventure of my company.

One of main adversaries of the globalization movement had been Thomas L. Friedman. With his book 'The world is flat,'[5] he had proclaimed that globalization would slowly but steadily create one market and eventually, an increasingly connected world in which the ease of doing business internationally would improve continuously. However, despite Friedman's forecast, international companies doing business in unexplored markets still face high levels of uncertainty and some of the world's toughest conditions. For example, most unexplored and emerging countries perform poorly in the World Bank's Ease of Doing Business surveys,[6] having constraints in the business environment such as practices of the informal sector, corruption, underdeveloped health care, poor infrastructure, political instability, lack of access to finance, lack of skilled labour,

[1] Hochberg et al. (2015).

[2] The Economist (2015), Jayaram et al. (2010).

[3] Åkesson (2018, p. 14).

[4] Idem.

[5] Friedman (2005).

[6] https://www.doingbusiness.org/en/rankings.

and economic instability due to high dependence on global commodity prices and regulations.[7]

Under these conditions of uncertainty and complexity, failure is quite common. In fact, MNCs incur indirect losses of thousands or even millions of dollars. Productivity may fall; customer and supplier relations may get damaged, leading to a lower market share and it may even lead to a discredited corporate reputation.[8] Staff relocation also comes with high costs and in addition, failure and withdrawal from international assignments can be very costly for the international management staff members themselves, in terms of diminished self-esteem and interrupted careers.

I must admit, with the wild strike of our employees, we had started to the feel the heat. We started to understand that the savvy companies, the ones that can exploit the opportunities in far-away markets successfully, the ones that are able to avoid wasting money, squandering time, and frustrating employees, these companies should have some serious risk management measures in place.

Culture and Soul Searching

The question for Silva and his management team was where to start with building a robust risk management system.

One of the things that stood out for us was the fact that during the spontaneous strike of the frontline workers, the alignment of the employees had been amazing. Not one of them provided us with any insight into the situation or even picked up the phone when we tried to reach out. Every single individual had acted in a perfect communal way, for the benefit of the collective. The community's secret sauce that turns intent into accomplishment had been present among all frontline employees, driving them to act together as a team and refusing to give up. It was clear that we had a challenge at group level.

The Indian American economist and professor Ghemawat went against the notion of Friedman on the large-scale interconnectivity of markets and

[7] Malfense Fierro (2015).

[8] Hochberg et al. (2015).

business.[9] He developed the CAGE Distance Framework, which distinguishes four fields of distance among countries and among business units throughout the world:

- Cultural distance.
- Administrative/governance distance.
- Geographical distance.
- Economic distance.[10]

All four of them bare their own risks, and for Silva, it was clear that he needed to concentrate on the large cultural risks they faced, especially regarding closing the gap and creating collaboration between management and their local, Angolan workforce.

Even after everything had been settled and even after my prompting, we never received any real answers or found out what transpired exactly. The gap between their world and my world hit me in the face; it seemed we were living in different realities. It was at this stage that I fully realized that we were dealing with cultural difference and that our risk was indeed cultural in nature.

It proved not to be an easy task for an international company like the one Silva was working in, to come to terms with the cultural complexity of its surroundings. Willing to look the lion in the mouth and to make sure he was on the right path, Silva posed himself and his surroundings some, what he called, 'soul searching questions.'

If only we would be able to learn from this event and amplify this (Angolan) community wisdom within our corporation, we might even be able to transform the risk into a strength. After all, people are most happy and productive when they can be themselves and be part and parcel of the same reality. For me, as Country Director, therefore, it is obvious and fair to say that I had an economic interest in mitigating this risk. At the same time, I was curious and very interested in getting to know my surroundings and my employees better. Before we would reach such a level, however, we needed to know how apt we actually were to face this challenge. We had some serious soul searching to do and we posed ourselves a few very probing questions:

[9] Ghemawat (2009).

[10] Ghemawat (2001), Lem et al. (2013).

1. *Is the company's management team blinded by some of the stereotypes that are so often promoted about Africa's local employees?*
2. *Is our management model and leadership style suitable to the actual social context and do we have enough cultural awareness?*
3. *Are we sure that all employees know and feel the company objectives, strategy, mission, critical tasks, and values, in the pursuit of efficiency and quality?*
4. *Do our interventions bring down barriers and build bridges to improve collaboration inside the company?*

I thought about the answers to these questions deeply. Yet, I was not on my own. I had intriguing conversations with both Angolan and expat colleagues from my personal and business networks, we had several meetings and talks within the management team and, at this stage, a few individual conversations with some of the frontline workers. The answers to the questions, generally, painted a rather bleak image of our cultural competence and savviness.

The rhetorical questions posed by Silva will not be answered in detail here. They were posed to create a self-awareness and the following paragraphs will provide some of the findings of Silva, while he was contemplating and dialoguing both with himself, his management books, and his environment.

The Cultural Blind Spot

Question 1: Is the company's management team blinded by some of the stereotypes that are so often promoted about Africa's local employees?

Overall, cultural differences are regularly forgotten by business leaders or dealt with only at superficial level. There seems to be a certain blind spot. The idea that business is business, that every human being, in his strife to optimize profits, will make the same 'objective' choices, is abundant. Schneider (et al.) also observe that for many managers and management scholars, "Management is management. (…) Management practice is considered to be scientifically engineered and therefore able to transcend national boundaries."[11] This idea is also driven by so-called best practice global companies, giving the impression that there is one 'best

[11] Schneider et al. (2014, p. 8).

Fig. 2.1 The onion with several layers

way'. But according to Schneider and numerous other scholars, this is a myth. Hofstede[12] has shown in not to be misinterpreted language that global management doesn't exist as one single entity and management finds very different forms in various contexts (Fig. 2.1).

One of the main reasons behind this cultural blind spot is that the deeper cultural patterns find themselves at unconscious levels. Each culture in itself is a complex system, often depicted as an onion with several layers. According to Schein,[13] we can distinguish three layers:

1. Artefacts and behaviours (the outer layer; observable through our senses).
2. Beliefs and values (the middle layer; knowable through interviewing).
3. Basic assumptions (the core of the culture; only detectable through inference).

Especially the latter are hard to detect, as these basic assumptions are hidden from sight. Cultural programming is learned through our social upbringing and being learned so early in life, most people are hardly aware of their own deep cultural values and assumptions. These are so 'logical' to them, they assume automatically that others think, feel, and act in the same way, whether in their personal lives or in professional life.

[12] Hofstede (1993).

[13] Schein (1985).

It is very common that knowledge about a different culture remains restricted to the outer layers, leading to rather obvious information and the emergence of superficial stereotypes. Training people, to raise awareness and understanding, does help, but one cannot expect people to display completely new behaviour, and there is a high probability that in many, and especially in stressful, situations, people automatically revert to their original behaviours.[14] If companies that are working with a diverse workforce truly want to leverage cultural differences, making use of innovative points of view and complementary forces, it is often crucial to raise awareness about the unconscious, basic assumptions, to surface and to study the deeper layers of culture, and to institutionalize certain processes in order to mitigate and use the differences.

The Global Strategy Company Profiles

Question 2: Is our management model and leadership style suitable to the actual social context and do we have enough cultural awareness?

On the one hand, MNCs strive towards standardization of products and policies from HQ, partly unconsciously and partly for efficiency reasons. At the same time, there are demands for local adaptation, such as local taste, local marketing, and local policies regarding country requirements and employees.

One model from the management literature, that spoke to our imagination while thinking through this soul-searching-question, was the classification of Perlmutter. He described three global strategic profiles, defining the relationships between HQ and subsidiaries: ethnocentric, polycentric, and geocentric,[15] *together known as the EPG model. These distinct typologies influence and shape diverse aspects of multinational enterprises, including structural design, strategy, and resource allocation, and, most of all, management processes.*

The typologies in the EPG model are described as follows.

In an ethnocentric company, the policies and procedures emanate from the top. The systems of beliefs and values from HQ are usually considered morally superior to all others. Key management positions, such as all heads of Management, R&D, Finance, Sales, Human Resources, and

[14] Deresky (2007).

[15] Perlmutter (1969), Hill (2005), Schneider et al. (2014).

Operations, are mostly filled by nationals from the country where HQ is situated (expats).[16]

Within a polycentric profile, on the other hand, the local preferences and techniques are found most appropriate for the local market, and therefore, policies and procedures are implemented in a local manner. It is assumed that host-country nationals are most suitable to deal with the local conditions. Therefore, the staffing policy in this constellation is such that local people fill the most important management positions.

In a geocentric profile, the focus is on a more world-oriented approach. It does not show a bias to either HQ or host-country preferences. It spotlights the significance of doing whatever it takes to better serve the organization, where "policies and procedures are developed with input from both HQ and subsidiaries, as well as across subsidiaries."[17] Since different cultures do come together, it seems that within this approach there's more exchange and negotiation taking place, taking up time but with the best chance for the optimal solutions to various situations. Examples for the key staff functions are, from company HQ: the heads of Management, Finance, and R&D; and from the host country the heads of Sales, Human Resources, and Operations.

Additional to these three company profiles, Perlmutter, together with other authors, later describes a fourth approach, named as region-centric, which relies on local managers from a particular geographic region to handle operations in and around that area.[18] Here we find a regional office (for instance for Benelux, North America, Southern Africa, or Eastern Europe), and this office serves as a buffer between overall HQ and host-country subsidiaries. The EPG model then turns into the EPGR model.

In our case there was no regional office. But we did look around our management table and we established that we all came from Portugal, although one of us was of mixed upbringing and one other manager had been living in Angola for decades. But all in all, we had to admit we were a European management team, staffed mainly by expats. Surely this way we would miss out on information and on a diversity of viewpoints within our subsidiary.

[16] Perlmutter & Heenan (1974).

[17] Schneider et al. (2014, p. 243).

[18] Wind et al. (1973), Hodgetts & Luthans (2003).

Looking at the organization of western MNC's worldwide, many executives have a predilection for the standard controlling systems, formal hierarchical structures, and command economies. There is no MNC today whose executives can honestly say that ethnocentrism does not exist in their organization.[19] Most of the management books and theory at business schools the world over do come from the US or the Western world in general, and worldwide accountancy and advisory use the same models over and over again.

Management literature stresses the importance of the global mindset of international managers, of enacting geocentric leadership.[20] *The search for these managers and leaders is an ongoing challenge for all multinational organizations and companies. Almost all international companies and other organizations face high costs due to the transfer of the staff, usually named expatriates, moving overseas. Although enabling a higher degree of control and improved communication between subsidiary and HQ, there is always the risk that this staff is culturally incompatible and unable to fit into the new environment. Some managers seem to adapt in an almost chameleon-like manner to different cultures, whereas others cling (sometimes desperately) to their habits and their national approaches. Also, it is known that the factors spouse and family issues are very critical for the success of an international assignment.*

In 2001 it was estimated that one in seven UK managers fail on international assignments, and this figure is even higher for US managers, with an estimated failure rate ranging from 25 to 40 percent.[21] Furthermore, the degree of failure does not follow a clear 'fit or unfit' distinction. Home country staff may remain on the assignment but withdraw psychologically, which also incurs indirect losses for their companies, including poor decision-making, damaged customer relations, and discredited corporate image and reputation.

We concluded that we needed to move from a somewhat ethnocentric side towards the geocentric side of the scale. I was very grateful to the company for all the opportunities and support they had given to me and to the subsidiary. For the time being, however, all our HR policies and our so-called

[19] Barlett et al. (2008).

[20] Osland & Bird (2006), Cabrera & Unruh (2012).

[21] Marx (2001, p. 5).

best practices emanated from HQ and/or from Anglo-Saxon management literature and it seemed it needed an extra step.

In these rather ethnocentric settings, the corporate direction, such as strategy, mission, values, and goals, is often established in the company headquarters with a single-country perspective. They are often hardly known, let alone felt and 'owned', by middle management, foremen, and frontline employees of a subsidiary. Silva, talking to his employees and thinking back to the occurrence of the strike, concluded that this general tendency was true for his subsidiary as well, thus simultaneously answering the third question (*Are we sure that all employees know and feel the company objectives, strategy, mission, critical tasks, and values, in the pursuit of efficiency and quality*?) in the negative.

Flexibility and Information Flow

Question 4: Do our interventions bring down barriers and build bridges to improve collaboration inside the company?

Hill observed that the centralized approach of ethnocentrism and standardization from HQ may result in a lack of flexibility and responsiveness to different markets, which may prevent the subsidiaries from reaching their full potential.[22] The hands-on information from the bottom has a very hard time reaching the top. This is portrayed in Fig. 2.2.

As a result, and as was mentioned in the introduction, corporations run the risk to pay an ignorance tax: the established standards do not adapt to specific cultures when operating globally and top management decisions are often uninformed by the collective intelligence of the company.[23] Decisions are often taken in offices far away from employees that are the guardians of key information.

Here we are at the core of the challenge we were facing. We had a serious issue concerning the bottom-up information flow, which became so painfully clear during the frontline employee's strike.

It is very common that due to the hierarchical layers, important data from the frontline does not reach the management board. In the next

[22] Hill (2005).

[23] Deresky (2007).

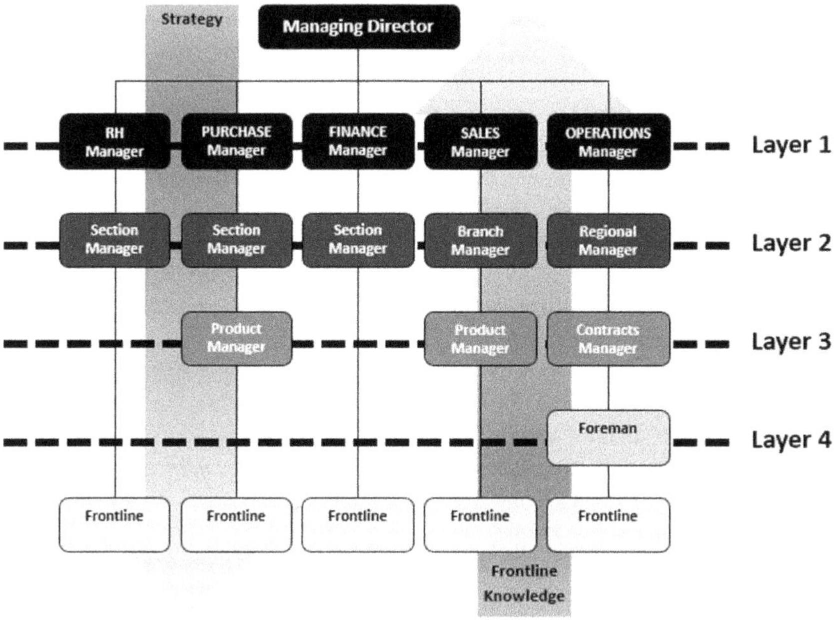

Fig. 2.2 Company knowledge and information flow—before intervention

chapter, we will see that in this particular case, it was not merely the tendency of ethnocentrism, but added to it was the cultural difference in itself, between the Portuguese and Angolan cultures, which exacerbated the challenge of bottom-up information flow.

The Ultimate Goal of Silva

So far it has been established that the subsidiary in this case study, despite good intentions, finds itself in a rather ethnocentric space, that there is a deeply felt disconnect between management and employees and that management is slowly becoming aware of its cultural blind spot. After this soul-searching period, Silva laid out his ultimate goal for transformative change.

Slowly but steadily, we realized that we had a long route ahead, if we truly wanted to make the best of two worlds meet, between our Portuguese, Western-style company, on the one hand, and the Angolan culture of our employees, on the other. Many concepts were staring us in the eye: cultural awareness and interpretation, social-context knowledge, company culture, local responsiveness, company informal structure, information flow for improved decision-making, local workforce integration, geocentric leadership. By posing ourselves the soul-searching questions, reading our literature again, and having various conversations, we became aware that all these key concepts are far more complex than we had foreseen and could lead to misunderstanding and break-down of cooperation inside the company. We became convinced that 'culture neutral interventions,' such as hiring criteria, production processes, or planning strategies, have dangerous limitations in building effective co-operative bridges between cultures. Such practices do not take the unwritten rules of social culture into account, nor can they predict behaviour of managers or employees in various settings. All in all, these interventions are mostly not as 'neutral' as they seem. Managing truly in a geocentric fashion and finding culturally confluent solutions seemed to involve courage, much more work, and many steps into the future.

Our one-million-dollar question was what could we learn from the African management practices in general and from Angola specifically: How could we unleash the indigenous insights, integrate them into our structures and procedures, and improve our cultural-context leadership? How could we mitigate this cultural risk into an opportunity, possibly even a competitive advantage? To find answers to these questions, we decided to start in-depth cultural research, with the ultimate goal to develop a culture specific intervention, gluing the whole company together and transforming it into a culture-centred workplace, to support growth, and to drive performance. Our objective after the research was to embark on a transformative change process that would be vested in simple, genuine, and logical local concepts, easy to implement in a lasting way, and hopefully not relying on any fundamental change in behaviour from either side.

References

Åkesson, L. (2018). *Postcolonial Portuguese migration to Angola*. Palgrave Macmillan.

Barlett et al. (2008). *Transnational management: Text, cases and readings in cross-border management* (5th ed.). McGraw-Hill.

Cabrera, A., & Unruh, G. (2012). *Being global: How to think, act and lead in a transformed world*. Harvard Business Review Press.

Deresky, H. (2007). *A review of international management: Managing across borders and cultures* (6th ed.). Pearson Prentice Hall.
Friedman, T. L. (2005). *The world is flat*. Farrar.
Ghemawat, P. (2001, September). Distance still matters. *Harvard Business Review, 79*(8), 1–11.
Ghemawat, P. (2009). Why the world isn't flat. *Foreign Policy*. https://foreignpolicy.com/2009/10/14/why-the-world-isnt-flat. Consulted on 29 October 2019.
Hill, C. W. L. (2005). *International business: Competing in the global marketplace* (5th ed.). McGraw-Hill Irwin.
Hochberg, N., Klick, J., & Reilly, E. (2015, September 16). What companies have learned from losing billions in emerging markets. *Harvard Business Review*. https://hbr.org/2015/09/what-companies-have-learned-from-losing-billions-in-emerging-markets. Consulted on 5 October 2019.
Hodgetts, R. M., & Luthans, F. (2003). *International management: Culture, strategy and behaviour* (5th ed.). McGraw-Hill Irwin.
Hofstede, G. (1993). Cultural constraints in management theories. *The Executive, 7*(1), 81–94.
Jayaram, K., Sanghvi, S., & Riese, J. (2010, June). *Africa's path to growth, sector by sector*. McKinsey and Company. https://www.mckinsey.com/featured-insights/middle-east-and-africa/africas-path-to-growth-sector-by-sector. Consulted on 5 October 2019.
Lem, M., van Tulder, R., & Geleynse, K. (2013). *Doing business in Africa, a strategic guide for entrepreneurs*. Bereschot International B.V.; Partnerships Resource Centre at RSM Erasmus University Rotterdam and Netherlands-African Business Council.
Malfense Fierro, A. C. (2015, July 31). After Obama comes the big challenge for Africa's entrepreneurs. *The Conversation*. https://theconversation.com/after-obama-comes-the-big-challenge-for-africas-entrepreneurs-45383. Consulted on 5 October 2019.
Marx, E. (2001). *Breaking through culture shock: What you need to succeed in international business*. Nicholas Brealey Publishers.
OECD. (2011). *Economic Diversification in Africa: a Review of selected Countries*. Paris: OECD Publishing.
Osland, J., & Bird, A. (2006). Global leaders as experts. *Advances in Global Leadership, 4*, 125–145.
Perlmutter, H. (1969). The Tortuous evolution of multinational enterprises. *Columbia World Journal of Business, 4*(1), 9–18.
Perlmutter, V. H., & Heenan, A. D. (1974). How multinational should your top managers be? *Harvard Business Review, 52*(6), 1–13.
Schein, E. H. (1985). *Organizational culture and leadership*. Jossey-Bass Publishers.

Schneider, S., Barsoux, J. L., & Stahl, G. K. (2014). *Managing across cultures* (3rd ed.). Pearson Education Limited.
The Economist. (2015, January 22). *Foreign investment of Africa: A sub-Sahara scramble*. https://www.economist.com/business/2015/01/22/a-sub-saharan-scramble. Consulted on 5 October 2019.
Wind, Y., Douglas, P. S., & Perlmutter, V. H. (1973, April). Guidelines for developing international marketing strategies. *Journal of Marketing, 37*(2), 14–23.

CHAPTER 3

Contemporary Tradition and Modernity in Africa

Abstract The second chapter of Part I recounts the context in which this story is told. Africa below the Sahara faces the daunting challenge to create wealth for its peoples and to deal with its disruptive history: slave trade, followed by a relatively short period of true colonialization, independence, and the remaining strive for decolonialization. Africa may be characterized by an emerged reality of 'having a double version of everything': traditional and modern. While by no means static, nor mutually exclusive nor free from power inequalities, we can detect the search for 'traditional' indigenous forms of leadership, management, and organization and the efforts to reconcile a mosaic of cultural logic and institutions. Some talk about the search for hybrid forms, others call it confluence and in this story about the Portuguese subsidiary in Angola, the questions will be posed what are the rather static, essentialized aspects of culture and which flexible, performative aspects of culture can in the end be distinguished (both from Angolan and Portuguese sides)?

Keywords Tradition and modernity · African management philosophy · Decolonialization · Ubuntu · Hybrid · Performative

A. Vonk and V. F. Silva, *Cultural Confluence in Organizational Change*, Palgrave Studies in African Leadership,
https://doi.org/10.1007/978-3-031-45403-5_3

Historic Roots of Tradition and Modernity

To put the case of Silva and his organization into full perspective, it is indispensable to zoom out and set the stage in the wide African[1] cultural environment in terms of management and organization. One of the most important aspects to point out about this context is that, apart from the enormous variety among the African nations and regions on this huge continent, there is a cross-cutting phenomenon which can be found throughout sub-Saharan Africa, and which is intensely described by both African and foreign scholars and philosophers. This is the notion that the past centuries seem to have created a reality of (and a necessity to manage) different, sometimes conflicting, systems of logic. At first sight, it is as if the Africans have a 'double version' of everything. There is (what is often locally called) a 'traditional' way and a 'modern' way of handling life.[2]

Hence, there is traditional governance (with elders, chiefs, kings, and/or courts) and there is the modern state with all its layers and institutions. There is traditional law and there is the modern law, and both are being practiced finding justice. There is traditional religion (animism) and 'modern' religion (in the African context: Christianity and Islam), all very much alive. For health-related issues, people can turn to traditional and to modern medicine; and on many occasions, one can find traditional and modern dress, food, language, marriage, education, even security institutions like the police and army. Last but not least: there is a formal (modern) economy and a large, increasing informal economy,[3] which is governed by more indigenous rules.

Silva: As a subsidiary from a Portuguese company, we naturally collaborated with the 'modern' side of Angolan society. We were obviously part of the formal economy. But with our employees, the cultural complexity was part of our reality as well. The more we learned, the more it made us wonder what we actually knew about Angolan management and Angolan leadership.

It has been argued that this disconnection between the traditional and modern aspects of African life and finding solutions to bridge the gap is

[1] In this book, geographical labels such as 'African' or 'Western' are used as defined by Metz: "to refer to features that have been salient in a locale for a substantial amount of time" and "relative to other parts of the world" Metz (2022, p. 7).

[2] Gyekye (1997).

[3] For descriptions of Informal economy in South African townships, see Alcock (2015, 2018).

one of the major challenges of sub-Saharan Africa as a whole. In fact, it is seen by some (Africans and outsiders alike) as one of the reasons why this large and diverse continent seems to be lagging in terms of wealth creation and providing prosperity for its peoples.[4] Obviously, the main origin of such dualism is to be found in the history of colonialism. On top, almost the whole continent has been colonized for a relatively short amount of time, compared to other colonized territories in the world.

After centuries of trade and a very disruptive slave trade, organized mostly from coastal fortresses and areas, European powers actually conquered the interior from the end of the nineteenth century until the 1920s. Decolonization started from the 1960s. "In most cases the colonial system continued only for some forty years after conquest and remained unchallenged only for twenty-five."[5] Dia reminds us that "In Latin America independence followed several centuries of colonial rule. During this period, pre-colonial formations and attachments lost their potency because of extermination, cultural assimilation and massive immigration from Europe and Africa. (…) Direct colonial control was briefer in Africa (…) and was only episodically associated with settler colonialism."[6]

That is not to say that there had not been fierce interference, causing political, economic, and social instability before colonialization. In the case of Angola, for instance, Candido shows that in the hinterland of the city Benguela, the trans-Atlantic slave trade spread violence and vulnerability, causing the collapse and migration of existing polities, emergence of new ones and continuously changing affiliations, vassalage, negotiations, and wars.[7] She also points to the fact that the Portuguese had started to colonize some spots in the interior, with a few fortresses, creating new and partly mixed communities and controlling some of the most important trade routes (dominantly of slaves). Yet, the Portuguese only controlled 10% of the territory in 1904 and the borders of the colony were only realized in the 1920s.[8]

[4] Vansina (1992), Iguisi (2014), Dia (1996), Senghor (1964), Gyekye (1997), van Pinxteren (2018), etc.

[5] Vansina (1992, p. 18).

[6] Dia (1996, pp. 38, 39).

[7] Candido (2013, pp. 237–312).

[8] Åkesson (2018, p. 7).

This turbulent period was followed by a relatively short period of colonialization, in which the whole continent of Africa was turned upside down. It was characterized by fierce fighting at some places (either against a colonizer, among different African peoples or caused by the world wars), an imposed superstructure and shattered or subdued indigenous institutions at others. Even if there was no fighting going on, "colonial administrators were extremely powerful and influential in shaping political Africa, as we know it today,"[9] while "African chiefs were expected to behave at once like monarchs to their people and unquestioning subjects to the Empire."[10] This was also true for the so-called *Sobas*, the traditional chiefs in Portuguese Angola, where both the trade of slaves and extreme forms of forced labour continued long after the slave trade had officially been abolished. Many Sobas could barely avoid serving as "assistant in the requisition of workers."[11] Speaking generally about Africa, Kiggundu states that "during colonialization the various colonial powers first destroyed or denigrated local institutions and management practices and then replaced them with their own administrative systems, out of the belief in Western cultural, biological and technological superiority over Africans."[12]

Although some Africans had long before started to get educated into the European traditions (either forced or by their own interest, and by formal education or by missionaries), this assumed larger proportions during colonialization. After independence, in many countries a new, still relatively small, and European educated elite took over the very young state structures. Many with strong ideals but removed from the masses, and the structures they inherited were largely built on oppression. According to Young, attempts to build governance structures that truly fitted in with the indigenous culture and traditions were hardly made.[13] Eze and Van der Wal mention that many of these first post-colonial leaders may have been too Pan-Africanist, neglecting to fill the void that needed new institutional nation building within their new geographies.[14]

[9] Jordans et al. (2020, p. 33).

[10] Jallow (2014, p. 10).

[11] Jerónimo (2015, p. 40).

[12] Kiggundu (1991). In: Nkomo (2011, p. 376).

[13] Young (1986).

[14] Eze & Van der Wal (2020).

The masses, in the meantime, were culturally disoriented, described so intensely by the famous Nigerian writer Chinua Achebe in his book 'Things fall apart."[15] In the case of Angola, violence and disorientation were even worse, with a bloody independence war of 13 years, followed by a civil war, which lasted from 1975 to 2002.

Instability and distress, as well as religious, educational, and cultural influence, had created sociocultural transformation, yet many indigenous institutions had not disappeared. According to the historian Vansina, describing the post-colonial period for Africa, "even the basic criteria for perceiving reality are not commonly held by all, let alone that there would be consensus on the existing choices, objectives, priorities, standards, ethics and legitimacy on any issue."[16] The Ghanaian philosopher Gyekye described it as follows: "African nations have since the dawn of post-colonial rule been groping through an ideological labyrinth."[17]

Apart from fighting and the strive and success of the independence movement, there was, and still is, a growing body of intellectual reaction to the oppression and loss of dignity, caused by colonialism and neo-colonialism. Psychiatrist Fanon described how colonialism had brought about processes of assimilation and self-alienation in Africans.[18] Mudimbe argued that "the reformation of the native's mind was designed to socialize Africans to despise their history, culture and themselves—their very blackness"[19] and Stuard Hall writes about the internalization of inferiority.[20] In the 1930s, still during the colonial period, a mix of young black people, mostly from French colonies and studying in Paris, started the movement by the name Négritude,[21] raising black awareness and revolting against the notion that the black race was seen and treated as backward and uncivilized.[22] With the Martinican Nardal sisters

[15] Achebe (1958).

[16] Vansina (1992, p. 9).

[17] Gyekye (2004, p. 73).

[18] Fanon (1967, 1968).

[19] Mudimbe (1988). In: Nkomo (2011, p. 368).

[20] Hall (1994). In: Nkomo, p. 369.

[21] The term was coined by Martinican poet and activist Aimé Césaire. In: Nkomo (2011, p. 368).

[22] See Nardal (Jane) (1929), Nardal (Paulette) and Sharpley-Whiting, (2014), Césaire (1935–1966), Léon Damas (1937–1972), Leopold Senghor (1939, 1948, 1971).

providing the "intellectual and institutional infrastructure,".[23] Léopold Senghor became one of the most prominent African in their midst, later to become the first Senegalese president at independence. Senghor advocated the celebration of African customs and notions. The movement wanted to reclaim the aesthetics, dignity, and identity of Africans all over the world.[24] All in all, a positive identity of Africans needed to be rediscovered and restored and this agenda remains recognizable over the rest of the past century, moving from anti-colonialist thought into postcolonial thought.[25] It continued and continues to play a large role in, what is called, African management philosophy that followed (from the end of the twentieth century onwards), all the way into the present, in the adoption of the Black Lives Matter movement and the current call for decolonialization of various aspects of public life.

African Management Philosophy

African management philosophy originates from the thought that Africa's development will not be successful unless it is based on or incorporates authentic, indigenous management systems. Dia states that Africa is crippled by one "overarching theme: an institutional crisis (…) a structural disconnect between formal institutions transplanted from outside and indigenous institutions."[26] As Iguisi has shown, "the different management theories of motivation, leadership, organization in the forms that have been developed in the west, do not or partially fit culturally in Africa." According to him "there is the need for the application of anthropological concepts to the field of human resources and appropriate management theorizing in Africa."[27] Gyekye points out that there are many elements in the traditional philosophy of African logic to harness. "African notions (…)," he writes, "have value systems that could form the material fabric for constructing appropriate and viable ideologies."[28]

[23] Blain and Gill (2019, p. 76). See also Sharpley-Whiting (2000, pp. 8–17).

[24] Mbeki (1998). In: Nkomo (2011, p. 375).

[25] Ahluwalia (2001).

[26] Dia (1996, p. Vii).

[27] Iguisi (2014, p. 74).

[28] Gyekye (2004).

This idea, in part also (but certainly not only) stimulated by the end of apartheid in South Africa, resulted in a search for authentic African management and leadership forms and has led to a large and very interesting body of literature. It is impossible and far beyond the objective of this book to give a comprehensive overview, but a short summary of this body of literature can be found in an article of Nkomo[29]:

> "Whereas Western management thought is said to advocate eurocentrism, individualism and modernity, 'African' management thought is said to emphasize traditionalism, communalism, co-operative teamwork and mythology (Mutzabazi, 2002; Nzelibe, 1986). Edoho (2001) also argues that communalistic life is the centrepiece of 'African' personality (…). 'African' management thought is also said to be characterized by a strong belief in an individual's relation to nature and supernatural beings and connections between the individual and ancestors (Mbigi,, 2005, Nzelibe, 1986). (…) Africa's ancient empires in Ghana, Mali and Shongai and Oyo are given as historic evidence of the existence of effective management systems and leadership. While power was centralized, the success of a leader (..) lay in his (sic) capacity to listen well and to put the community's interest first (Mutabazi, 2002; Ngami, 2004)."

Apart from such broad descriptions, different indigenous concepts and philosophies are being studied and promoted, such as *Ujamaa* (collectiveness, in Tanzania); the *Kgotla* (Village Assembly and community decision-making in Botswana); *Indaba* (African leadership, based on respect for competent and experienced elders); and especially *Ubuntu* has become very important and appealing to many, both scientists and practitioners. Ubuntu can be called one of the centrepieces of African Management philosophy. According to Battle,[30] the concept originates from the Xhosa expression *Umuntu ngumntu ngabanye abantu*, which means that everyone's humanity is ideally expressed in relationship with others. Mbigi states that the literal meaning of Ubuntu is 'I am because you are—I can only be a person through others.'[31] In Ubuntu management, therefore, the relationships between people at all levels are key, which may at times be conflicting with western logic. What may be

[29] Nkomo, 2011, p. 376.

[30] Battle (1996, p. 99). In: Molose (2019, p. 31).

[31] Mbigi (2000, p. 6). In: Molose (2019, p. 31).

perceived as nepotism in the West, may be morally correct and be of aid to the manager at the African workplace. In Ubuntu, "the servant leader is the chief agent of striving towards harmony in community"[32] and inside the company. "In the moral universe of Ubuntu, humanity is conceived of as one large family that is bonded together by reciprocal ties of love and loyalty. This is, of course, an ideal conception towards which we should forever strive, both in family, governance as well as at the workplace."[33]

According to Newenhan-Kahindi, "the word Ubuntu is found, with slight variations in pronunciation, over a wider geographical and social region in east, central and southern Africa. For example, the largest tribe in Tanzania, the Sukuma, uses the word *Bantu*; the Zulu tribe in South Africa uses *Abantu*; Sesuto people in Southern Africa use *Batho*; the Herero people in Namibia use *Avandu*; in central Africa, it is *Ngumtu*, *Kubuntu*, and *Edubuntu*; and the Swahili people in East Africa use it as *Watu*, again implying togetherness or people as being together."[34] Ubuntu is accepted as an African value system, also describes as African "humaneness—a pervasive spirit of caring and community; harmony and hospitality, respect and responsiveness."[35] In management terms, this means that the organization and leadership should resonate with the needs of the employees, not at individual level, but as a community. It stresses the importance of understanding employee workgroup cohesion and belonging to optimize team unity and performance.[36]

One of the latest offshoots of the search for indigenous values and organizational principles is the recent moral theory of communal relationships, based on African values, by Metz. He composes this moral principle around harmony and friendliness: building relationships in which one identifies and exhibits solidarity with others. Applied to business ethics, rather than contract-based relationships between employer and employees, he stresses the importance of forging community in the workplace, "which by present ethic means creating, sustaining and

[32] Khoza (2006, pp. 58–59).

[33] Khoza (2006, pp. 58–59).

[34] Newenham-Kahindi (2009, p. 92).

[35] Mangaliso (2001, p. 24).

[36] See also Ndaba (1994), Mbigi & Maree (1995), Mbigi (1997), Horwitz et al. (2002), Nussbaum (2003), Newenham-Kahindi (2009), Eze (2010), Molose (2019), etc.

enriching bonds of identity and solidarity amongst workers and ideally between them and managers/owners too."[37]

Confluence of Narratives

While Vansina, in his article with the title 'A past for the future,' states that it will be the traditional logic of Africa that will ultimately dominate the cultural landscape of Sub-Sahara Africa, most authors foresee a blend of originally 'African' and 'western', or 'foreign' thought and institutions. Dia states that "neither total institutional transplant (external enclaves) nor traditional fundamentalism (conservatism) is a viable alternative for Africa's development."[38] It was Coleman who wrote already back in 1954 about a syncretistic (merging) movements, apart from the traditionalist and the modernist movement. Even Senghor, being firmly in favour of returning to African cultural values, had written later in life his famous words of "*enracinement et ouverture*"[39]: the deep-rooted African institutions should be combined with an openness to the world.

Iwowo, a Nigerian scholar at London University, speaks about African leadership and asks herself what the next step should be. "While there is need to re-appraise leadership development in Africa which is still heavily influenced by Western/Anglo-Saxon leadership theory, sweeping ourselves back to a 'glorious African past', as the African Renaissance thought school would have us believe is the solution, is also not realistic. We need to relate to the 'now', which is shaped by both history, our colonial past, and also influenced by present day interactions with the rest of the world."[40] Therefore, Iwowo talks of the 'third space' or Hybrid model, with a combination of Indigenous Knowledge (IK) and Mainstream Theories (MT) within African Societies[41] (Fig. 3.1).

At the same time, this search for the hybrid, third space raises some issues of concern. One problem is that it may turn a blind eye to the relationships of power among the different components and bodies of thought which are supposed to blend. Jackson as well as many other

[37] Metz (2022, p. 219).

[38] Dia, (1996, p. 33).

[39] Senghor, (1964)

[40] In: Jordans et al. (2020, p. 50), Iwowo on Skype with Jordans.

[41] Iwowo (2015, p. 424).

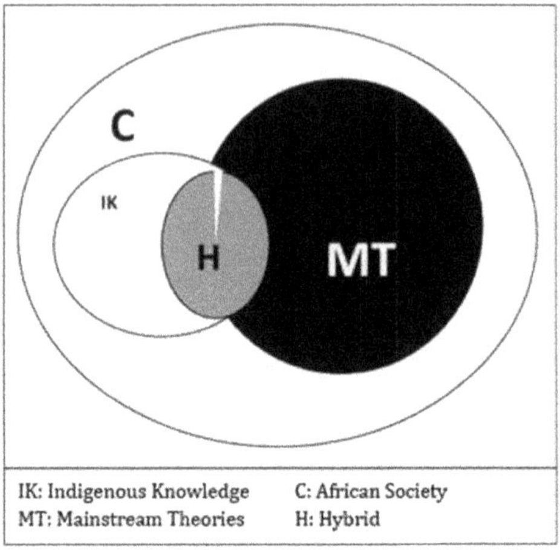

Fig. 3.1 The Hybrid Space (*Source* Iwowo [2015, p. 424])

post-colonialists stand up for integrating "power relations, imposition of institutions and knowledge, and resistance"[42] into the research and analyses being executed. The famous question of Spivak needs to be posed over and over again: "Can the subaltern speak?".[43]

In the current story of the Portuguese multinational in Angola, this question is pertinent. As mentioned in the previous chapter, both the Country Director and most of his management team were dominantly Portuguese, while foremen and frontliners were dominantly Angolan, and this poses questions about the racial and power relation between the two groups. Åkesson studied the Portuguese/Angolan relationships in Angola from 2013 to 2015, during the period of influx of Portuguese into Angola, caused by economic hardship in Portugal and economic boom in Angola. She analysed the consequences of this reversal of migration and need. Although she observed both continuity and changes in the relationships between the former colonized and colonizers, she came across "continuous power of the colonial hierarchies" and a "remarkable continuity between the social relations of labour."[44] In her book, she mentions numerous situations where the Portuguese are still the

[42] Jackson (2013, p. 25).

[43] Spivak (1988).

[44] Åkesson (2018, p. 133).

managers, or "masters" and the Angolans their subordinates. According to her, this is partly caused by lingering old colonial ideas (from both sides) which have a long-standing and profound effect in post-colonial Angola. "The deep inequality—but also violent intimacy—characterizing colonial times is all but bygone. The two partners are meeting again on partly new grounds, but embodied memories from the past shape present patterns of behaviour. Which in turn create new feelings of superiority and of revolt."[45] On top, Åkesson mentions that post-independence development is also linked to processes that go beyond colonial continuities, for instance the failure of the Angolan party-state to construct "a decent educational system and reliable institutions, and this obviously has had disastrous consequences for its citizens' possibilities to compete with the Portuguese in the labour market in Luanda."[46] Relations of power, therefore, need to be taken into account in any study of hybridity.

The second concern with the concept of hybridity is that the naïve observer may assume two opposite, rather closed bodies of logic that contribute notions into the hybrid space of 'traditional' and 'modern' aspects. Once again, we need to point at the vastness of the African continent and all the different histories, cultures, and experiences, possibly feeding into this space in a large variety of ways. More fundamentally, there is the risk of describing identity "in purist, essentialist and oppositional terms."[47] Eze and Van der Wal state: "The pre-existing binarism traps us within an Afro-pessimistic outlook, of a people 'hopelessly imprisoned in the past' (…) making African identity the 'other' of modern reason and progress."[48] They would like to recover alternative narratives of African identity, make room for multi-layered identities, and acknowledge the internal capabilities of change and development.[49] "Tradition is (..) a history in the making," they write, "Historical tradition itself is not static but dynamic, as it exhibits elements of continuity in its dialogue with the past, the present and future contingencies."[50] While Gikandi still

45 Ibid., p. 129.

46 Ibid., p. 135.

47 Eze (2014, p. 240).

48 Eze & Van der Wal (2020, p. 201), Gikandi (2010, p. 9).

49 Gikandi (2010, p. 9).

50 Eze (2010, pp. 3, 5).

uses the word 'hybridity,' others prefer to use the word convergence,[51] and Eze proposes to speak of a confluence of narratives, providing room for internal regeneration, autonomic growth, and negotiation between simultaneously co-existing, developing, and interacting tales.

Consequently, Eze prefers to focus less on the *essentialist* conception of cultural phenomena (in his view rather dogmatic and static) and more on their *performative* nature: are the concepts and ideas open-ended; do they have the ability to produce new meaning and "enabling conceptual frames"?[52] And: "Can they create space in which every encounter is a recreation of the self and where dialogue is always key?".[53]

The Ghanaian/English philosopher Appiah confirms the importance of dialogue.[54] He speaks of practical-oriented intercultural dialogues that need to take place to bridge possible gaps, and which need intercultural competence. Eze, analysing the intercultural dialogue further, states that it is necessary to acknowledge what we do *not* have in common, recognizing and including the 'other,' thereby becoming vulnerable and at the same time, gaining equality.[55]

Interestingly enough, Geschiere (et al.)[56] even decomposed the mere notions of 'modernity' and 'tradition', showing their nature as historical constructs with so much external overlap and internal contradictions, that they hardly hold as distinct bodies of logic. This meticulous work illustrates the complexity, the width, the flexibility and the confluence of cultures. Yet at the same time the concepts of modernity and tradition appeal to the imaginations of many Africans, judged by the body of literature around the subject. Both in their essentialist, and in their possible performative nature, they do form part and parcel of the narratives in Africa. De Witte writes that "we can also not simply dismiss these notions, seeing that (...) the notion of 'modernity' is very powerful and pervasive."[57] This is true for the notion of 'tradition' as well. Although by no means simply inherited from the past without autonomous progress,

[51] See Horwitz et al., (2021, p. 1).

[52] Eze (2010, p. 126).

[53] Interview with Eze in Shadid (2021).

[54] Appiah (2006). In: Müller (2023).

[55] Eze (2022, p. 62).

[56] Geschiere et al. (2009).

[57] Witte de (2012, p. 84).

neither static nor homogeneous, it should be noted that tradition has a positive and compelling connotation in many circles in Africa, where deeply engrained ethical norms do revolve around an African (for instance Angolan, Mbundu, Luanda, etc.) identity. On the surface, an average Angolan youngster today might seem to reject the traditions, and he or she may behave and dress very 'modern.' Yet it might often be much harder for him or her to truly go against the ruling of a Soba, a traditional chief, than to do the same thing against a civil servant or a politician.

Complementary Notions

This book follows and underpins Eze in his ideas of confluence of cultures, multi-layered identity, and the performative nature of cultural phenomena. After all, culture is, more often than not, used and described in a static and condescending manner, flattening peoples and individuals into false, often negative stereotypes, and paying only lip service to its depth, the wide internal variety and multiple identities, its wealth of different narratives and its ability to adapt and develop.

At the same time, however, it is of no use to fall into the trap of, what the Bennett's called, minimization,[58] pretending that cultures don't exist or where differences are swept underneath the carpet. In other words, it is not helpful to 'cancel' culture and be blind to cultural variance, and it is necessary to acknowledge that it is simply impossible to write about culture without at least some form of generalization or essentialization. After all, culture is a group phenomenon; it describes a group of people and therefore will always generalize up to a certain extent. Nkomo adds, quoting Banerjee: "'unbridled anti-essentialism' can end up disempowering and denying the agency of colonized peoples to resist domination by the West."[59] Stuard Hall recognizes that identity is a matter of becoming as well as being and "argues that scholars do not have to choose between difference and hybridity but instead recognize that both are valid."[60] Collective identities and cultures hold a fascinating and astonishing wealth of wisdom and responses to the demands of the human condition. They hold images and visions that move and inspire people to belong and to

58 Bennett & Bennett (2002), Bennett (2017).

59 Nkomo (2011, p. 379), Banerjee (2000, p. 10).

60 Stuard Hall (1994). In: Nkomo (2011, p. 380).

act. Ethnographically studying these cultures and identities does bring the field forward, and it will not help to throw out the baby with the bath water.

It is on this slippery road, then, that this book explores a tiny part of this cultural wealth, by showing both its essentialist and its performative nature and flexibility, both on the Angolan and on the Portuguese side, and in one, specific, case study. The point of departure is that in order to analyse (multinational and national) companies in Africa and to find the best solutions to their management challenges, many different points of view are needed. It needs the ethnographic 'essentialist' description of what *is*, expressed by the people in this specific story in time and space, as well as the binary notions, like modern and traditional, and like the dimensions of national cultures, as described by Hofstede and many others, which will be introduced in the next chapter. It needs the account of the confluence taking place, as well as the question what has been performative in this case? These different ways of studying culture and management do not contradict each other, they complement each other. This book is in all respects a call for a confluence of narratives: combining management practice with scientific thought; combining western with African ideas; combining storytelling with scientific debate; and combining the modern and the traditional in both essentialist and performative manners.

The main argument is that there are useful ideas and concepts to be found within African 'contemporary tradition,' which are or can become 'modern' and play a role in the world of multinational management and vice versa. The story answers the call of Nkomo and many others, who have asked for more descriptive (rather than prescriptive) research "that examines how leaders and managers in organizations in Africa are responding to the dual pressures of globalization and local needs,"[61] with the mission to tell the story of a Portuguese manager in an Angolan context, and to add one interesting case study to existing literature.

[61] Nkomo (2011, p. 379), See also Iguisi (2014 p. 74), Iwowo (2015), Gyekye (1997, 2004), Bhengu (2011), Lessem & Nussbaum (1996), Dia (1996, p. 76).

References

Achebe, C. (1958). *Things fall apart*. William Heinemann Ltd.

Ahluwalia, P. (2001). *Politics and Post-colonial Theory: African Inflections.* London and New York, NY: Routledge.

Åkesson, L. (2018). *Postcolonial Portuguese migration to Angola*. Palgrave Macmillan.

Alcock, G. G. (2015). *Kasinomics*. Tracey McDonald Publishers.

Alcock, G. G. (2018). *Kasinomics revolution*. Tracey McDonald Publishers.

Appiah, K. A. (2006). *Cosmopolitanism: Ethics in a world of strangers*. Allen Lane.

Banerjee, S. B. (2000). Whose land is it anyway? National interest, indigenous stakeholders, and colonial discourses. *Organization and the Environment, 13*(4), 3–38.

Battle, M. (1996). The ubuntu theology of Desmond Tutu. In I. Hulley, L. Kretzchmar, & L. L. Pato (Eds.), *Archbishop Tutu: Prophetic witness in South Africa* (pp. 93–105). Human & Rousseau.

Bennett, J. M., & Bennett, M. J. (2002). *Intercultural communication for practitioners*. Zürich University Press.

Bennett, M. J. (2017). Constructivist approach to intercultural communication. In Y. Kim (Ed.), *International encyclopedia of intercultural communication.* Wiley.

Bhengu, M. J. (2011). *African economic humanism: The rise of an African economic philosophy*. Gowing Publishing Limited.

Blain, K. N. & Gill, T. M. (2019). *To turn the Whole World over: black women and internationalism*. University of Illinois.

Candido, M. (2013). *An African slaving port and the Atlantic World: Benguela and its hinterland*. Cambridge University Press.

De Witte, M. (2012). Buy the future now! Charismatic chronotypes in neoliberal Ghana. *Etnofoor, 24*(1), 80–104.

Dia, M. (1996). *Africa's management in the 1990's and beyond: Reconciling indigenous and transplanted institutions*. The International Bank for Reconstruction and Development, The World Bank.

Eze, C. (2014). Rethinking African culture and identity: The Afropolitan model. *Journal of African Cultural Studies, 26*(2), 234–247.

Eze, M. O. (2010). *Intellectual history in contemporary South Africa*. Palgrave Macmillan.

Eze, M. O. (2022). Interculturality as dialogical reciprocity in African and comparative philosophy. *Filosofie & Praktijk, 43*(3/4), 49–64.

Eze, M. O., & Van der Wal, K. (2020). Beyond sovereign reason: Issues and contestations in contemporary African identity. *Journal of Common Market Studies, 58*(1), 189–205.

Fanon, F. (1967). First truths on the colonial problem. *Toward the African Revolution* (H. Chevalier, Trans.). Penguin.

Fanon, F. (1968). *On national culture and the pitfalls of national consciousness. The wretched of the earth* (C. Farrington, Trans.). Grove Press.
Geschiere, P., Meyer, B., & Pels, P. (Eds.). (2009). *Readings in modernity in Africa*. Indiana University Press.
Gikandi, S. (2010). Foreword: On Afropolitanism. In J. Wawrzinek & J. K. S. Makokha (Eds.), *Negotiating Afropolitanism: Essays on borders and spaces in contemporary African literature and Folklore* (pp. 9–11). Rodopi.
Gyekye, K. (1997). *Tradition and modernity: Philosophical reflections on the African experience*. Oxford University Press.
Gyekye, K. (2004). *The unexamined life: Philosophy and the African experience*. Sankofa Publishing Company.
Hall, S. (1994). Cultural identity and diaspora. In P. Williams & L. Chrisman (Eds.), *Colonial discourse and postcolonial theory: A reader* (pp. 392–403). Columbia University Press.
Horwitz, F. M., Cook, F. L., & Kamoche, K. (2021). Human resource management in emerging markets: Theoretical perspectives for understanding contexts. In E. Parry, J. M. Michael, & C. Brewster (Eds.), *The Oxford handbook of contextual approaches to human resource management*. https://doi.org/10.1093/oxfordhb/9780190861162.013.6
Horwitz, F. M., Kamoche, K., & Chew, I. K. H. (2002). Human resource management in Africa. *International Journal of Human Resource Management, 13*(7), 1019–1041.
Iguisi, O. (1994). Appropriate management in an African culture. *Journal of Management in Nigeria, 30*(1), 16–24.
Iguisi, O. (2014). African values for the practice of HRM. *Beykent University Journal of Social Sciences, 7*(1), 56–77.
Iwowo, V. (2015). Leadership in Africa: Rethinking development. *Personnel Review, 44*(3), 408–429.
Jackson, T (2013). *Reconstructing the Indigenous in African Management Research. In Management International Review 53*, 13–38. https://doi.org/10.1007/s11575-012-0161-0
Jallow, B. G. (2014a). The case for African leadership case studies and leadership in colonial Africa: An introduction. In B. Jallow (Ed.), *Leadership in colonial Africa: Disruption of traditional frameworks and patterns*. Palgrave Macmillan.
Jerónimo, M. B. (2015). *The 'civilising mission' of Portuguese colonialism 1870–1930*. Palgrave Macmillan.
Jordans, E., Ng'wena, B., & Spencer-Oatey, H. (Eds.). (2020). *Developing global leaders: Insights from African case studies*. Palgrave Macmillan.
Khoza, R. (2006). *Let Africa lead: African transformational leadership for 21st century business*. Vezubuntu.

Kiggundu, M. N. (1991). The challenges of management development in Sub-Saharan Africa. *Journal of Management Development, 10*(6), 32–47.

Lessem, R., & Nussbaum, B. (1996). *Sawubona Africa: Embracing four worlds in South African management*. Zebra Press.

Mangaliso, M. P. (2001). Building a competitive advantage from ubuntu: Management lessons from South Africa. *The Academy of Management Executive, 15*(3), 23–33.

Mbeki, T. (1998). *Africa: The time has come*. Tafelberg.

Mbigi, L. (1997). *Ubuntu: The African dream in management*. Knowledge Resources.

Mbigi, L. (2000). *In search of the African business renaissance: An African cultural perspective*. Knowledge Resources.

Mbigi, L., & Maree, J. (1995). *The spirit of African transformation management*. Sigma.

Metz, T. (2022). *A relational moral theory: African ethics in and beyond the continent*. Oxford University Press.

Molose, T. (2019). The equivalence of Southern African heritage of Ubuntu. In H. H. Kazerooney, A. Stachowicz-Stanusch, & W. Amann (Eds.), *Advancing African knowledge management and education* (pp. 27–48). Information Age Publishing.

Mudimbe, V. Y. (1988). *The invention of Africa: Gnosis, philosophy, and the order of knowledge*. Indiana University Press.

Müller, L. (2023). Human wellbeing in intercultural philosophical perspective: A focus on the Akan philosophy of Wiredu, Gyekye, and Appiah. In B. Bateye, M. Masaeli, L. Müller, & A. Roothaan (Eds.), *Well-being in African philosophy: Insights for a global ethics of development* (pp. 13–49). Lexington Books by Rowman & Littlefield.

Nardal, J. (1929). Internationalisme noir. In S. B. Diagne (2010). http://plato.stanford.edu/archives/spr2014/entries/negritude/. In E. N. Zalta (Ed.). (2014). *The Stanford encyclopedia of philosophy*.

Nardal, J. (2002). Black internationalism. In T. D. Sharpley-Whiting (Ed.), *Negritude women* (pp. 105-107). University of Minnesota Press.

Nardal, P. & Sharpley-Whiting, T.D. (2014). *Beyond Négritude: Essays from Women in the City.* State University New York Press.

Ndaba, W. J. (1994). *Ubuntu in comparison to western philosophies*. Ubuntu School of Philosophy.

Newenham-Kahindi, A. (2009). The transfer of Ubuntu and Indaba business models abroad: A case of South African multinational banks and telecommunication services in Tanzania. *International Journal of Cross-Cultural Management, 9*, 87–108.

Nkomo, S. M. (2011). A postcolonial and anti-colonial reading of 'African' leadership and management in organization studies: Tensions, contradictions and possibilities. *Organization, 18*(3), 365–386.
Nussbaum, B. (2003). Ubuntu: Reflections of a South African on our common humanity. *Reflections, 4*(4), 21–26.
Sharpley-Whiting, T. D. (2000). Femme negritude: Jane Nardal, La Depeche africaine, and the Francophone New Negro. In *Soul: Critical Journal of Black Politics & Culture, 2*(4), 8-17
Senghor, L. S. (1964). *On African socialism* (M. Cook, Trans.). Pall Mall.
Shadid, S. (2021). *Genealogies of philosophy: Michael O. Eze*. Blog of the American Philosophical Association. https://blog.apaonline.org/2021/01/08/genealogies-of-philosophy-m-onyebuchi-eze/. Consulted on 8 August 2022.
Spivak, G. C. (1988). Can the subaltern speak? In C. Nelson & L. Grossberg (Eds.), *Marxism and the interpretation of culture* (pp. 271–313). Macmillan.
Van Pinxteren, B. (2018). *African identities: A new perspective*. African Studies Centre.
Vansina, J. (1992). A past for the future? *Dalhousie Review, 68*(1–2), 8–23.
Young, C. (1986). Africa's colonial legacy. In R. J. Berg & J. S. Whitaker (Eds.), *Strategies for African development* (pp. 25–51). University of California Press.

PART II

Cultural Research: Etic and Emic Approaches

It is often assumed by expat managers that cultural insights can be obtained reading some available literature about the local culture, published in press or on-line; attending some seminars and workshops; and having a few conversations with past expats that lived and worked in the host country. These insights are very valuable as an introduction to the subject, yet they provide either a very generic overview or a handful of anecdotes. Culture, however, is a complex matter and it invited me to a fascinating lifelong learning journey. It is the application of the generic overview; the interpretation of observations, conversations, and experiences and their translation and implementation in both practical and strategic terms, that may ultimately lead to a competitive advantage.

After the wild strike and the first step of soul searching and awareness raising, described in Chapter 2, Silva was about to start research, with the intention to take him down the path of far better cultural understanding. The research can be divided into two approaches of study into the field of cultural variation, and both will be used, as Silva also did himself. In his case it is not possible to speak of phases since one did not necessarily follow or precede the other; the different perspectives influenced each other and a discovery in one field led to new insights in others. Life can be messy, and insights can emerge from every corner. However, for the sake of clarity, these two approaches and their outcomes will be outlined separately, in Chapters 4 and 5.

Chapter 4 deals with cross-cultural psychology or possibly a better phrase: comparative culturology.[1] It is a field of study whereby it is possible to *compare* different cultures. It falls within the category of what is called the *etic* approach: analysing cultures from the outside. "People are often too involved in what they are doing (...) to interpret their cultures impartially."[2] Therefore, the etic approach takes a helicopter view (as much as possible), allowing for the comparison between different value systems. In this case, the etic research will be used predominantly to understand the gap between Portuguese management and the Angolan workforce.

To find local concepts on organization and leadership, one needs an *emic* approach. Emic cultural research "investigates how local people think."[3]For instance, it points out how the Angolan people, and with them the employees of the company, perceive and categorize the world themselves: their rules for behaviour, what has meaning for them, and how do they imagine and explain things. Silva applied one of the management principles of the successful 'Toyota Way': *Genchi Genbutsu*, or 'Go and see for yourself,' and delved into local custom. The results of this part of his research can be found in Chapter 5. At the end of this chapter, there is an overall conclusion of the cultural research of Part II, describing the most important drivers and insights, the elements that Silva will use for the practical application, which will be described in Part III.

[1] Minkov et al. (2023, forthcoming).

[2] Kottak (2006, p. 47).

[3] Idem.

CHAPTER 4

The Hofstede Model: Understanding a Multicultural Environment

Abstract The difference between etic and etic research is shortly explained, and the chapter sets off with a discussion on the (dis)advantages of etic research. Used in a positive way and with care, it gives us a chance to compare cultures and, in this case, is executed through the cultural dimensions of Hofstede. The different basic values of Angola, Portugal, and the USA (where most management literature originates) are compared, and they explain the situation leading up to the strike as well as provide clues as to how to proceed into the organizational change process. Fully understanding the main cultural differences between Portuguese management and Angolan frontliners concerning power distance, collectivism, and uncertainty avoidance (giving form to the so-called pyramid culture) provide a lot of understanding of the strike and the behaviour of the employees. Furthermore, these differences topped up with the cultural similarities between Angola and Portugal, in terms of a tender culture, striving for dialogue and consensus, and short-term orientation, with high respect for traditional wisdom, form interesting points of departure for the change process.

Keywords Etic cultural research · Pyramid culture · Application of Hofstede · Jealousy in Africa · Classical communitarian debate

A. Vonk and V. F. Silva, *Cultural Confluence in Organizational Change*, Palgrave Studies in African Leadership,
https://doi.org/10.1007/978-3-031-45403-5_4

This chapter is dedicated to the etic cultural research, used to be able to make comparisons between cultures. There is a large body of research and thought in the field of etic research and the comparison of cultures along various aspects and features.[1] One of the most comprehensive and evidence-based studies of cultural values was conducted by the late Professor Geert Hofstede, which will be used here.[2] The model will be shortly explained first, after which it is necessary to delve into a thorough discussion on both its shortcomings as well as its strengths, since this and other etic research have received quite some criticism and should be handled with care. In the subsequent paragraph, the model will be explained in more detail based on the relative and average differences among Angola, Portugal, and the USA. Taken in with the necessary precautions and added with other etic research, it does provide Silva with interesting seedlings for the change process that he envisages. In the last paragraph, the model will be applied to the strike and its surrounding (lack of) communication, throwing an insightful light on the 'different realities' that had hit Silva in the face: What had most probably happened and how can he overcome the fact that mutual trust has received a blow within his company?

Introduction of the Model

After extensive research, spread out over 45 years, Hofstede (and other scholars collaborating with him) found six main areas of cultural variance. These areas of difference can be considered six basic dilemmas of the human condition. Each culture tends to deal with these basic dilemmas a bit differently than others. Hofstede talks of the six dimensions of national culture, each one measuring unconscious basic assumptions or, as he called them, basic values. Hence, he places them in the core of the 'cultural onion'. The six dimensions represent preferences for certain circumstances or conditions, measured in large groups (mostly countries). The dimensions and their dilemmas are the following:

[1] Kluckhohn and Strodbeck (1961), Smith et al. (1995, 1996), Schwartz (1994, 2006), Hall and Hall (1990), Inglehart and Baker (2000), House et al. (2004), Minkov (2007), Meyer (2014); etc. For an overview: see Minkov (2014) or Holtbrügge (2022).

[2] Hofstede (1980a) and Hofstede et al. (2010).

- Power Distance Index (PDI)—How to deal with power.
- Individualism vs. Collectivism (IDV)—How to deal with group relations.
- Masculinity vs. Femininity (MAS)—How to deal with performance and care.
- Uncertainty Avoidance Index (UAI)—How to deal with the unknown.
- Long-Term vs. Short-Term Orientation (LTO)—How to deal with past, now, and future.
- Indulgence vs. Restraint (IVR)—How to deal with pleasure.

Being based in empirical research and with statistical data (predominantly based on the answers of a worldwide employee satisfaction survey while he was working for IBM, added with other research and the UN World Value Survey), Hofstede developed for each dimension a scale from zero to hundred, each country scoring differently on the various dimensions. According to Hofstede, the national scores on the dimensions are relative, they can only be used meaningfully by comparison to each other.

In Table 4.1 the scores for Angola (for the frontline workers) and Portugal (the Country Director and the larger part of management) are presented. The USA is added since most management literature (and subsequently the underlying assumptions of many management models and 'best practices') stems from this country. These scores will be explained in detail, in the third paragraph of this chapter.

Hofstede first published his dimensional framework in his classic book *Cultures Consequences* in 1980, with four dimensions at the time. Other

Table 4.1 Country scores on dimensions of national culture

	PDI	*IDV*	*MAS*	*UAI*	*LTO*	*IVR*
Angola	83	18	20	60	15	83
Portugal	63	27/48	31	99	28	33
USA	40	91	62	46	26	68

Sources Hofstede et al. (2010) and Finuras (2013)[3]

[3] Angola had not been part of the original study of Hofstede but was researched by Paulo Finuras in 2010/2011 and published in his dissertation (2013). Finuras also found a different score for Portugal on IDV, which will be discussed later.

scholars found the other two dimensions and after collaboration, these dimensions were added to the model. It has received both a lot of praise and considerable criticism ever since. Many have built on to the dimensions-paradigm[4] while others have critically examined the model.[5] Before explaining the dimensions and applying the model to the specific case of Silva and the frontliners, this debate needs some serious attention, taking a somewhat scientific trip away from the main story. Albeit interesting for all, readers who are eager to read about the practical findings and solutions found by Silva may want to pass over to the next paragraph.

Advantages and Disadvantages of the Hofstede Model

The Hofstede model has six binary scales, each with two oppositional sites, carrying a large risk of alienation and exclusion. It is frequently stated, for instance, that the model overgeneralizes and labels the individual, based on his or her country of origin, in a harmful manner. Others state that the Hofstede dimensions do not only label the individual, but also set whole countries aside: flourishing societies with an enormous riches in culture and variance in rituals, heroes, art, institutions, values, knowledge, histories, and a wide variety in thought and behaviour. The idea that Hofstede (and other etic researchers with him) breaks all of this down into specific numbers on a few binary scales can be quite disturbing. People feel hurt, stereotyped, and trapped in a deterministic, essentialist prison from which there seems no escape.

A different, yet somewhat similar reaction is frequently found among social scientists, studying culture from a more qualitative and emic point of departure. Minkov states that the Hofstede "paradigm tends to be ignored by many sociologists and most anthropologist (…), who are ill prepared for the idea of quantifying aspects of culture."[6]

Completely on the opposite side, the Hofstede model of cultural dimensions has been welcomed as a real paradigm shift in cultural studies.

[4] For instance, Trompenaars (1993), Smith et al. (1996), GLOBE in: House et al. (2004), Meyer (2014), Minkov (2007–2022).

[5] For instance, Schwartz (1994, 2011), McSweeney (2002), Kwek (2003), Triandis (1982), and Ailon (2008).

[6] Minkov (2014, p. 220).

The model has been embraced for bringing cultural variation back to its core and for creating a relatively neutral language for complex and sensitive differences. As such, it has been applauded for the "great advances it has made in unbundling the black box of culture."[7]

Answering the critics, Hofstede and other etic researchers stress that *all* forms of behaviour, values, and beliefs are found in *all* societies (either in different individuals and/or in different orders of preference), giving room for a wealth of cultural phenomena and for all possible narratives.[8] The figures on the scales are merely *tendencies*, he states. While dealing with human dilemmas, groups of people make slightly different choices in the complicated balancing act among different values. Hofstede measured these choices and found different *majorities* in different nations, based on empirical research and statistical analyses. Indirectly, one might make the comparison with the use of geographical labels in the recent work of Metz, mentioned in the previous chapter. Constructing an 'African' moral theory, Metz explains that he calls certain features 'African' or 'western' if they are "salient in a locale over a substantial amount of time" and "relative to other parts of the world."[9] As he argues, this is neither essentialist, since such features are not everywhere in Africa or in the West, nor non-existent in other parts of the world; nor is it constructivist, since they are mind-independent facts, found through independent research.

Etic researchers also emphasize that measuring the values of an individual is fundamentally different from measuring culture, which can only be done for large groups of people.[10] This means that the cultural values found for a specific country are by no means laid down into every individual of that society, although most individuals from that culture know how to deal with the majority values in their country. On top, it means that countries may have a similar score on a specific dimension, yet the way this tendency of preference of one basic value over another plays out and finds its way into behaviour or institutions, may differ largely. Hence, according to Hofstede, the model provides room for all kinds of narratives for individuals, organizations, and various groups within all countries.

[7] Williamson (2002, p. 1392).

[8] Hofstede (2001, p. 73; 2002).

[9] Metz (2022, p. 27).

[10] Further emphasized by Minkov et al. (2023).

The more essentialist part of the Hofstede model may not so much be found in the variety of narratives, practices, and values found in each society, as well as in its assumptions on change and development. According to Hofstede, rapid change can and does occur in the outer layers of the onion (which he calls 'practices'). At the same time, however, he states that the deep, basic values do not change easily: it needs disruptive and/or long-term circumstances to change the unconscious fabric of a society, which is passed on endlessly and quite unconsciously from one generation to the next. This is a very challenging point of view to many scientists who prefer a more open-ended view on cultural phenomena. Beugelsdijk (et al.) have delved into this stability/change issue, by studying different generations (using data from the World Values Survey). They found that the deeper values of cultures do change. For instance, they found a worldwide decreasing score for power distance, while individualism is on the rise. At the same time, their data show that these changes are absolute rather than relative in nature. In other words, if the whole world is moving in a certain direction (for instance lower power distance), the relative differences between countries seem to remain largely intact.[11]

Another reproach to Hofstede is that there could be a euro-centric bias in his model. Hofstede, with his IBM research, discovered the first four dimensions and two of these, Masculinity and Uncertainty avoidance, do tend to be more useful to distinguish among European countries than among African countries (albeit still recognizable at times).[12] The fifth dimension was found with the aid of a survey that was constructed by Chinese scholars.[13] Noorderhaven and Tidjani did the same exercise for the African continent.[14] They conducted research with a list of African values, constructed from the suggestions of African scholars in Africa and African students abroad (40 people in total). The dimensions they thus started out with were: 'Human Goodness,' 'Rules & Hierarchy,' 'Importance of religion,' 'Traditional wisdom,' 'Sharing,' 'Jealousy,' 'Collectivism,' and 'Societal responsibility.' Some of these dimensions turned

[11] Beugelsdijk et al. (2015). See also Beugelsdijk and Welzel (2018); Blog 1 of Hofstede (2019).

[12] See also Taras et al. (2012).

[13] Chinese Culture Connection (1987).

[14] Noorderhaven and Tidjani (2001).

out to correlate closely with some of the Hofstede dimensions and/or with some governmental or economic parameters, but there was no new, 'African' dimension found, as occurred with the Chinese survey. Unfortunately, the survey was executed in seven African countries only (Angola was not among them) and the planned follow-up research did not take place due to lack of finance. In this and coming chapters, some of their findings will be discussed whenever appropriate.

Besides these studies, there's a lot more etic research to be found. Authors like Minkov and Holtbrügge provide extensive overviews and discussion, which go way beyond the content of this book.[15] Recently, Minkov and Kaasa brought the six dimensions of Hofstede back to two dimensions: Individualism/Collectivism and Monumentalism/Flexibility, the last one being close to the Hofstede Long-/Short-term orientation.[16] This Minkov-Hofstede model, as they call it, needs more research and deprives the practitioner of some of the handles of the Hofstede tool, but these two dimensions are indeed very salient in the current story as well.

Twenty-five years after Hofstede's original publication, Kirkman (et al.) conducted a comprehensive review of 180 studies, which tried the Hofstede dimensions on several areas of international management, like conflict management, HRM, reward allocation, leadership, negotiation, and others. In conclusion, Kirkman and his co-authors agree with Smith and Bond that most studies "have sustained and amplified [Hofstede's] conclusions rather than contradicted them" and that "most country differences predicted by Hofstede were supported."[17] Another ten years later, the same researchers conclude that "clearly, breaking out of this conventional culture paradigm will be tough."[18] They point towards exciting new routes for researchers to take. In this book, one of their suggestions is being followed, namely, not to (try to) break away from the paradigm, but to complement it with emic research.

The ongoing debate on Hofstede's findings proves the robustness of the model on one side, yet sends out a clear warning, on the other: the

[15] Minkov (2014) and Holtbrügge (2022).

[16] Minkov (2018) and Minkov and Kaasa (2022).

[17] Kirkman et al. (2006, pp. 307–308), Smith and Bond (1999, p. 56). See also Drogendijk and Slangen (2006).

[18] Kirkman et al. (2017, p. 3).

model should only be used with care. Firstly, the essentializing, stereotyping and alienation of individuals, countries, or whole continents, lie just around the corner. Hofstede's work can easily be misused or misinterpreted, and he sends this warning out himself, distancing himself from a rigid use of the dimensional scores, saying this may well take place "in the eyes of the beholder."[19]

Secondly, it is important not to get too hung up on scores and figures. Hofstede himself used to write on the blackboard for his students: "CULTURE DOESN'T EXIST"[20] and, after analysing various cultural studies, Smelser concludes that culture is in fact "in large part a construct."[21] Culture seems to share some characteristics with the concepts of tradition and modernity discussed in the previous chapter: they are appealing, observable, and influential, yet there appears to be a lot of overlap and internal inconsistency. Smelser: "It seems that any systemic effort on the part of an investigator to depict a society's culture will inevitably yield a significant measure of incoherence – incompleteness, illogicality, contradiction- in his or her rendition."[22] Therefore, although the cultural dimensions of national culture of Hofstede do depict certain averages on certain topics, and although Minkov and Kaasa claim objective existence of at least their two dimensions, it is indispensable to understand the fact that all values and behaviours occur in each country. Hence, the scores do by no means provide a good explanation for every specific situation.

Finally on this list of warnings and risks, it is important to realize that the model only describes differences and similarities in country averages. When people from various backgrounds meet and interact, however, more often than not there is also a power relation between them: one may have more power to influence the interaction than the other. The Hofstede model does not take these power relations between the different groups into account, whether in the world in general or in a specific setting where negotiation or dialogue takes place.

[19] Hofstede (2002, p. 1358).

[20] Hofstede (2002, p. 1359).

[21] Smelser (1992, p. 23).

[22] Idem, p. 24.

On the positive side, rather than using the dimensions to box people in, they can also be used to create understanding.[23] In fact, the dimensions are used as a reflection handle by academics, business schools, and managers the world over. For many, the interpretation of the scores for each of these six dimensions provides predictions and insight into the tendencies of the people from a certain country as compared to others. Smelser states that a cultural description "should be assessed primarily on its explanatory adequacy or its usefulness as an explanatory element rather than on its significance as an empirical description."[24] As Venkateswaran & Ojha state: "By attempting to 'solve' the 'social problem' that cultural differences pose, by studying value differences among (…) different nations and working backwards to building a model that helps understanding the differences, Hofstede's work is eminently pragmatic. (…) In short, despite its weaknesses, the fundamental argument for the continued use of Hofstede's framework is its impact on practice and attempt to address real challenges in a global and multi-cultural economic context."[25] Despite its flaws, the model is widely accepted because, according to them, it provides "the 'best available explanation' for many cross-cultural issues, especially for practice. Critics should also appreciate what the framework explains, rather than focus on what it is unable to explain."[26]

Thus, the model can be used to manage expectations, to interpret otherwise incomprehensible situations, and to strategize better into the near and the far future. The dimensions can be used as a start for the necessary dialogue, rather than an end. Albeit sensitive, this conversation is imperative: "Research indicates that managers are ineffective in cross-cultural situations when they either deny having stereotypes or get stuck in them. Managers rated most effective by peers were those who admitted having stereotypes, using them as a starting point, but continually revising them as they gained more experience."[27]

[23] According to the film 'An engineer's odyssey,' creating understanding was the rationale for Hofstede when he started cultural research, after growing up during World War II. See Smit and Siegmund (2014).

[24] Smelser (1992, p. 23).

[25] Venkateswaran and Ojha (2019, p. 426).

[26] Idem, p. 425.

[27] Scheinder et al. (2014, p. 18).

Therefore, the following paragraphs will explain the model further, dimension by dimension, followed by applying them to the business case of Silva and his company. Rather than using the dimensional approach to alienate people, Silva used the dimensions to apprehend an (to him) obscure reality. After all, he couldn't make sense of his surroundings. He had the impression there was a mismatch on ideas what to do in times of crisis, between the Portuguese management and the Angolan frontliners, and mutual trust was severely challenged.

The Hofstede Dimensions of National Culture

Silva: An interesting paradox of cultural knowledge is that to clear the glass lens through which you can correctly perceive the surrounding environment, you must first dive below the surface to uncover insight. That insight involves more than awareness of variations in language, customs, and appearance. Core cultural differences are often invisible and unconscious, and therefore they cause the most surprises, confusions, and frustrations.[28]

Against the background of heeding the warnings of the previous paragraph, this paragraph will explain the dimensions of national culture, based on the country scores for Angola, Portugal, and USA, as shown in Table 4.1. It means that some of the cultural tendencies in these three countries will be sketched in very broad lines, in comparison with each other and with other countries in the world. In the paragraph thereafter, the dimensions will be applied to the company and the case of the wild strike. Furthermore, the resulting insights and understanding will serve the solutions found by Silva, his management team and frontliners, later in this story.

Power Distance

The first cultural dimension is the power distance index (PDI). This dimension expresses the degree to which the less powerful members of a society accept and expect that power is distributed unequally.[29] The fundamental issue here is how a society handles inequalities among its

[28] Ball et al. (2004).

[29] The definitions and explanations in this paragraph can be found in Hofstede et al. (2010).

people. The score that was established through research for Angola is 83, while the score for Portugal is 63. This indicates that more people in Angola, in comparison with Portugal, do assume a hierarchical order in society in which everybody has a place. In high PDI cultures, people of power averagely enjoy more privileges and those with less power generally show more respect and loyalty towards their leaders and to aged persons, and they will not easily contradict them. The rationale of the latter is that a leader and/or the elderly are assumed to have a far better view of the circumstances, have more wisdom through experience and therefore are better capable to conclude what should be done. In return for this loyalty from subordinates, the leader is often expected to take care of his/her people, like a benevolent father or parent.

This is truer for Angola than for Portugal, and the difference between Angola and Portugal of 20 digits between the two countries can be considered significant and will generally be (and was) felt at the workplace. The difference is even more significant with the USA (40), where an employee is supposed to take care of him/herself, expected to take initiative without being prompted, and to speak up in case they do not agree or have a different opinion during occasions like work meetings, performance reviews, etc.

Talking of power, note that this paragraph does not address the power imbalance between Portugal and Angola, as former colonizer and formerly colonized. Here the two cultures are dealt with and compared, each in their own right and describing how the superior/subordinate relationships are interpreted among their own people and within their own countries. As we've seen, the historical imbalance of power between these countries is also part of reality.

On the African continent as a whole, the PDI scores are relatively high. Naturally there are differences among ethnicities, where some groups or parts of societies are far more decentralized while others know a very hierarchical structure.[30] Looking at the similar scores throughout the continent though, one needs to be cautious in one's interpretation of this dimension, and it is important to add nuance to create clear vision.

Firstly, high PDI is not to be confused with authoritarianism. Especially in the traditional African power structures and at a local level, checks

[30] For an indication of PDI scores for more than 300 ethnic groups in Africa, see the thesis of Van Pinxteren (2018).

and balances were or are in place, as Gyekye[31] has pointed out. There are endless examples of courts, councils, and specific village or family gatherings all over the continent where people are invited to speak their minds freely. Such events take place in a specific space, organized for this purpose, often to find truth and to speak justice. During these sessions, it is very important for a leader to listen: "A good chief knows how to listen to the views and feelings of his people and with the finely tuned skills to restate those views, drawing in even those who differ, so that the decisions he articulates are echoed by all his subjects. The chief is the embodiment of the nation, his voice is born from all different voices."[32] Note that the good chief listens first and speaks last and note that it is he who takes the decisions. When the session is over, the power relations are often restored to their original settings, where subordinates are encouraged to refrain from commenting, unless granted permission. In other words, freedom of speech is, to an extent, ritualized or formalized.

Secondly, a large power distance may at times be challenging for, but is certainly not incompatible with, democracy. Countries in Europe like France (68) or Belgium (65) show this. Besides, "there is plenty of evidence indicating that humans have taken collective decisions together for most of their existence as a species,"[33] and the traditional spaces mentioned above are good examples of such forms of participation. Intellectuals like Cabral, Mondlane, and the first president of Mozambique Samora Machel, all from the Portuguese speaking parts of Africa, also share visions of direct democracy. Yet in practice, Graness perceives from the start of these new nations, an "inner tension between the affirmation of direct democracy and, at the same time, an assertion of (..) leadership (..)."[34]

Thirdly, in the past decade or two we tend to see changes in the way the continent of Africa as a whole is dealing with power, respect, and leadership. With education on the rise, the youth taking on positions and a revival of ritualized forms of participation like Ubuntu management, some countries and organizations in Africa are taking in a breath of fresh air. Based on the case study in this book, the last chapter will draw some

[31] Gyekye (2004, pp. 67–68).

[32] Dandala (2009, p. 267).

[33] Reiter (2021, p. 2).

[34] Graness (2016, p. 173).

interesting conclusions concerning the developments in relation to power and leadership.

A variety in points of view can also be found in African philosophical debate concerning the notions on personhood, which tie into this dimension of power distance.[35] Philosophers like Mbiti (Kenya), Menkiti (Nigeria), and Wiredu (Ghana) agreed that a human being *becomes* a person, through socialization of the individual in the community and through experience, fulfilling one's duties and maintaining relationships. Wiredu "thought that personhood in Africa implied more than just being born and that it was about achieving a certain social-ethical standard as one progressed in life."[36] Personhood, in this sense, is processual and therefore age-related: the older the person, the more respect is due and the more one is eligible to speak. In the words of Dandala: "age and life stages are an intrinsic part of the African world view. Both are associated with the acquisition of experience (...). It is not possible to speak about experience and downgrade age."[37] According to Gyekye (Ghana), on the other hand, one is already a person at birth, which represents a more egalitarian point of view.

For now, Hofstede points to the fact that, compared to many countries in the world, respect for leadership is considered correct behaviour in Angola. Speaking up is appreciated and encouraged in specifically designated spaces, but outside those places it is often uncalled for. This is true for Portugal as well, but generally speaking to a lesser extent than for Angola.

Individualism and Collectivism

On the index for individualism (IDV), Angola finds itself on the collectivist side of the continuum. According to Hofstede, collectivism represents a preference for a tightly knit framework in society in which individuals can expect their relatives or members of a particular in-group to look after them in exchange for loyalty. In individualist countries,

[35] Mbiti (1969), Menkiti (1984, 2006), Wiredu (2008, 2009), and Gyekye (1997). In: Müller (2023).

[36] Müller (2023, p. 24).

[37] Dandala (2009, p. 271).

people prefer a more loosely knit social framework. A society's position on this dimension reflects whether people's self-image is defined in terms of 'I' or in terms of 'we.' In collectivist societies the building and preserving of good relationships is key and in order to maintain harmony, communication is often indirect and contextual.

This is the only Hofstede dimension which defines 'the West' vis-à-vis the rest of the world: the so-called western countries (i.e. (north) western Europe, USA, Canada, Australia, and New Zealand) score relatively individualist, while almost the entire rest of the world scores more on the collectivist side of the scale. It is also the dimension which is related to wealth. With a few exceptions, "IDV-COL distinguishes the cultures of the wealthiest societies, at the IDV extreme, from those of the poorest, at the COL extreme."[38] Hofstede adds that individualism is not a cause, but rather an effect of economic wealth.[39]

Africa has profound communal roots and at the same time it has been dominated by and is liberating itself from a more individualist colonizer. As a consequence, the continent is deeply contemplating the question how to reconcile the interests of the individual and the community in contemporary Africa. Within philosophy it is called the 'classical communitarian debate' and a large part of the perceived divide between modernity and tradition revolves around this opposition between individualism and collectivism. Müller writes: "Nevertheless, most African philosophers that contributed to the classical communitarian debate agree that the community should continue to be more significant for the individual than is common in the modern Western world, but on the other hand, they acknowledge that there is an ongoing need in African philosophy to develop a new equilibrium between the importance of the community and the development and well-being of the individual."[40]

In this debate, philosophers like Mbiti, Menkiti, and Wiredu take a more communal stance, emphasising community, ubuntu, and the importance of relationships in most African societies. On the other hand, Gyekye "argued against Menkiti's way of reasoning that a person is entirely defined by his or her community. He (…) felt that Menkiti

[38] Minkov and Kaasa (2022, p. 5).

[39] Hofstede et al. (2010, p. 140).

[40] Müller (2023, p. 13).

undervalued Africans' individuality and, consequently, he did not sufficiently recognize their free will, agency, dignity, rights, and autonomy."[41] He points out that private entrepreneurship and ownership as one of the more 'individualistic' characteristics of the African economic life since time immemorial. According to him, African communitarianism had fooled some regimes into socialist experiments after independence, but to his eyes, this system wasn't compatible with those aspects of African culture.[42] Although public or communal ownership is more salient in the more collectivist cultures, this is indeed by no means true for all capital goods or sectors, and these cultures are not incompatible with private ownership.[43]

Very interesting, in this respect, is the dimension of 'Jealousy,' which was formulated with the aid of African scholars. Jealousy seems to be a topic that surfaces often in conversations in various African countries. Noorderhaven and Tidjani found that the seven African countries studied are spread out over the entire scale of this dimension. Remarkably, they also found that the dimension correlates with the 'marginal propensity to save' and they write: "Cultures that see jealousy as an important driver in society, seem to be inclined to save a larger proportion of income increments. This implies there is a tendency to withstand the pressure to spend one's income, which may be more to the benefit of others."[44] In other words: these preliminary results seem to suggest that in some African cultures, people may be inclined to use the argument of others being jealous, as a pushback against a strong collectivist norm of sharing and communal ownership.

Returning to the communitarian debate, Metz, hailing from the USA and with strong affiliations in South Africa, provides moral status to the individual rather than the community.[45] Based on the notion of personal dignity, he takes the individual as point of departure. Yet he advances harmony and communality, meriting pursuit for their own sake, and he emphasizes the communal *relationships* among the individuals. Hofstede, finding high scores for collectivism in Africa, does not pose the

[41] Gyekye (1997, p. 54). In: Müller (2023, p. 23).

[42] Gyekye (2004, pp. 56–63).

[43] Boubakri et al. (2016).

[44] Noorderhaven and Tidjani (2001, p. 43).

[45] Metz (2022, pp. 100–101).

question, let alone provide an answer, to this either/or question: What is more important, the group *or* the individual. Nor is he concerned about a semantic discussion among the words collectivism, communal, or communitarian. His analysis and finding point to the fact that for most African peoples the community, relationships, and harmony are more important in comparison with many other peoples in the world, especially to the westerner. Within that interpretation, the collectivist nature of the African cultures at large is obvious, and this was also revaluated by the study of Noorderhaven and Tidjani. In the words of Mbigi: "Although African cultures display awesome diversity, they also show remarkable similarities. Community is the cornerstone in African thought and life."[46]

Portugal, as measured by Hofstede in the 1970s, is more on the collectivist side of the equation as well (27), with only a difference between Angola and itself of 9 digits. Yet the communal behaviour of the Angolan workforce was amazing for, and well noticed by Portuguese management. As mentioned, the reason for this perceived difference may lay in this specific situation or in the personalities of the persons. It's also plausible that Portugal's score may have changed over the years. Although Hofstede states that these deep cultural values change very slowly, we've also seen that there is indication that wealth does drift a society towards individualism.[47] With the score of Hofstede found in 1973, Finuras found an IDV score of 48 for Portugal in 2013,[48] pointing out that the GDP of Portugal pushed up from 1,748 USD per capita in 1973, to 21,619 USD in 2013. This indication of a cultural shift is supported by a recent study of Minkov and Kaasa, who find an IDV score for Portugal of 30, on a scale from −291 to 182.[49]

The difference between the USA and Angola on this index can hardly be larger, with the USA scoring very individualistic.[50] A society is relatively individualistic when the majority values the right of every individual to self-develop in (almost) any direction, allowing for more different

[46] Mbigi (2005, p. 75).

[47] Hofstede et al. (2010, p. 140), Beugelsdijk and Welzel (2018, p. 1498).

[48] Finuras (2013).

[49] Minkov and Kaasa (2022, p. 12).

[50] Although recent research by both Beugelsdijk et al. (2015) and Minkov and Kaasa (2022) suggests that the USA is slowly becoming less individualistic in relation to other countries.

lifestyles and extreme choices within one country. Individualism is not to be confused with egoism, as this is a character trait of an individual (with negative connotations). In the culture of an individualist country, people are encouraged from young age to ventilating their individual opinion freely and to communicate rather explicitly. Having both relatively low PDI and high IDV values as the underlying assumptions in most management literature, instruments, and practices from the USA, one can imagine this has a strong influence on leadership, decision-making, and internal communication. In fact, a difference in these dimensions has consequences for almost all structures, procedures, and processes within organizations.

Masculinity and Femininity

Looking towards the masculinity index (MAS), both Portugal (31) and Angola (20) score relatively low, and both countries are considered 'feminine,' meaning that most people have a preference for cooperation, modesty, and quality of life, rather than competition, assertiveness, and financial ambition. Both Portuguese and Angolan society at large may be more consensus-oriented than others.

The terminology of this dimension has been subject to fierce debate, especially in the USA, and Hofstede has dedicated a separate book on the issue. "Study of work goals *by gender* have shown again and again that other things being equal, men tend to stress ego goals more and women tend to stress social goals more (...) One can speak of "gender cultures" (...) The Mas/Fem dimension is the only one of the [then] five that produces consistently different scores for female and male respondents (...), except in very feminine countries; it is the only dimension associated with the values that play a role in the differentiation of gender cultures."[51] Hence, Hofstede follows his statistical findings and, you may say, he follows his own Dutch, upbringing with direct speech. By calling this dimension Mas/Fem, he 'calls the little beast by its name,' according to the Dutch expression. However, once more this created the feeling in many people that they are being boxed in and one can argue that by using this terminology, there is little space left for change, for feminism, and for developing varying ways to perceive male and female roles and

[51] Hofstede (1998, p. 11).

gender in general. Therefore, 'masculinity' versus 'femininity' might just as well be called 'tough' versus 'tender' cultures, or achievement-oriented versus solidarity-oriented cultures.

Opposite of the tender cultures of Angola and Portugal described above, tough cultures (like USA and many others) represent a preference in society for achievement, heroism, and (material) rewards for success. Society at large tends to be more competitive and reward systems within organizations reflect these values.

The relatively more tender, consensus-oriented character of both Angola and Portugal, in this case, may not have been part of the problem of the company, but such a similarity can be an important ingredient for the solution, so it will be interesting to keep this dimension in mind.

Uncertainty Avoidance

The uncertainty avoidance index (UAI) expresses the degree to which the members of a society feel uncomfortable with uncertainty and ambiguity. The fundamental issue here is how a society deals with the unknown: should one try to control the future or just let it happen and improvise when necessary? With an UAI score of 99, Portugal can be considered very uncomfortable with uncertainty and more resistant to change, compared to other countries in the world. Generally, countries exhibiting higher UAI scores maintain more strict codes of belief and behaviour, and it is possible to observe the need for rules, structure, and formalization to create certainty. Low UAI societies maintain a relative more relaxed attitude in which practice and common-sense counts more than principles and expertise.

The high score for Portugal may not necessarily be applicable to a (predominantly) Portuguese management team that has left the secure homeland for adventure in Angola. At the same time, the mere start and execution of this cultural risk management research and organizational change process can be seen as a positive effort to control reality and prevent future surprises and shock. Interestingly, it is even possible to recognize a relatively high UAI in the way the current book is organized. The book starts with chapters of theoretical explanation and background, before finally coming to the solution in Chapters 6 and 7. This inductive reasoning is often found in higher UAI countries. Cultures with a lower UAI are more practical and books, articles, and presentations often start with the solution.

More generally, the high UAI score for Portugal is often explained by pointing at its rather conservative culture; its extensive and detailed legislation; the importance of formality both in dress and in addressing others; its religious nature (putting your fate in the hands of God may sooth the anxiety of an unpredictable life); and other factors which go beyond the content of this book.

Overall, the UAI scores are not very high in sub-Saharan Africa (in contrast to the Arabic countries above the Sahara): between 44 (Mozambique) and 65 (Ghana). Angola, with a score of 60, found by Finuras, seems to score on the higher side compared to its surrounding nations and he relates this to its very long period of war: the independence wars from 1961 to 1975, immediately followed by a civil war which lasted until 2002.[52] Although it is often very hard to prove where these deep cultural values are coming from (obviously delving into geographical and historic reasons), one can imagine that if war makes living unpredictable, people may have a tendency to control other aspects of life and in case the war lasts long, the deeper culture may change along. In comparison with Portugal though, the uncertainty avoidance of Angola is low and the score for the USA is even lower, giving way for a practical, hands-on management culture in the last country with less need for structure than in other countries.

Long-term and Short-Term Orientation

The 5th dimension is called long-term orientation index (LTO). In principle, every society has to maintain some links with its past, while dealing with the challenges of the present and preparing for the future, and this dimension suggests that societies seem to prioritize these existential goals differently. In a very general description, societies who score low on this dimension, like Angola and Portugal, prefer to maintain time-honoured traditions and norms, encourage hospitality and generosity in the present, while viewing societal change with some suspicion. Those with a higher score, on the other hand, plan far ahead, encourage thrift and efforts in modern education as a way to invest in and prepare for the future.

This dimension was originally found in a study executed by cross-cultural psychologist Michael Bond, who invited Chinese scholars to draw

[52] Finuras, in speech, 21–8–2018.

up a list of basic Chinese values, creating a different set of survey questions.[53] Indeed, the Chinese (and some other Asian countries) score very high on this dimension compared to other countries. As we saw, this research inspired Noorderhaven and Tidjani, in collaboration with Hofstede, to suggest a similar exercise for Africa.[54] One of the dimensions, constructed from the suggestions of the African scholars, was called 'Traditional wisdom.' The outcome of this dimension correlated negatively and nearly perfectly with the dimension found in the Chinese survey,[55] pointing towards a relatively short-term orientation on the African continent. According to Minkov, "further study of the structure of values have shown that importance of 'wisdom' can be closely associated with the importance of honouring the past."[56]

Angolan culture may be called relatively short-term oriented, and it shows values related to hospitality and generosity: "the importance of doing favours for others that might be reciprocated in the future"[57]; and the attention to the past and the present above that of the future. The dimension is also closely related to, what Minkov and Kaasa call, Monumentalism (short term) and Flexibility (long term). Cultures in the first group tend to prefer stability and consistency. This also means that decisions in Angola are, compared to other countries, more often taken based on the way things were done in the past, rather than based on the plans for a far-away future or on a more flexible 'truth'.

Portugal (28), in the meantime, shows a short-term orientation score as well. Likewise with the tender character of both Portugal and Angola, it is the similarity of values which forms a good starting point for finding solutions and bridging the cultural gap. As we will see, it was the genuine interest in and respect for traditions which proved to provide common ground from which to depart. Needless to say, the *content* of the history and the specific traditions in place (in other words: the outer layers of the cultural onion) vary enormously between these countries. Hence, the necessity remained to exchange the content of these traditions and concepts, which can be found in the emic research in the next chapter.

[53] Chinese Culture Connection (1987).

[54] Noorderhaven and Tidjani (2001).

[55] See Minkov (2014, p. 223).

[56] Fischer et al. (2010). In: Minkov (2014, p. 223).

[57] Minkov (2014, p. 223).

Indulgence and Restraint

Finally, Angola and Portugal differ considerably on the sixth dimension, Indulgence Versus Restraint (IVR), with the scores of 83 for Angola and 33 for Portugal. These scores indicate that Angolan society allows far more free gratifications of basic and natural human drives related to enjoying life and having fun. Portuguese culture, on the other hand, tends to be more restraint according to these scores, portraying a society that suppresses gratification of needs a lot more, and regulates it by means of strict social norms. In restraint cultures, life is a serious matter, and the overall feel might be a bit gloomy. To get a hint of the Portuguese tendency to the restraint side of life with more emphasis on suffering than on enjoying life, one could listen to their beautiful, melancholic Fado music.

In this context, it is interesting to point out that on the African continent a large variance is observed within this dimension, spreading from 18 (Burkina Faso) to 84 (Nigeria) and many different scores in between. Presumably, some of these differences are caused by geography. It is not hard to imagine that one needs to be more restraint in dry areas, with only one harvest a year. Many people in Africa may also recognize the difference between East and West Africa, the latter one generally scoring more indulgent. This sixth dimension is relatively new though and the variety found so far would be a fascinating point of departure for far more research that needs to be done in the future.

Understanding the Organizational Dynamics and the Strike

After this general interpretation, these basic values can be applied further to the case study followed in this book. What do these cultural tendencies tell us about the workplace, the company, the flow of information, and the occurrence of the wild strike? Can the Hofstede dimensions help Silva in his interpretation of the situation which he finds incomprehensible?

As a starter, it has been observed already that the employees acted in a collective manner, they acted as a whole. In fact, not all of them abstained from picking up the phone during that very stressful weekend for management, but almost all of them did. The two who answered the phone didn't provide any information, making it clear to Silva where their loyalty lied. Although in most collectivist societies, the first allegiance goes to the extended family (and only to a lesser extent to colleagues), and although one can observe a dislike for strike-breakers all over the world, the solidarity that the Angolan team demonstrated was impressive to Silva and his team. It can be interpreted as behaviour that fits the collectivist character of their culture, in which loyalty to the group is generally highly valued. Collectively they succeeded in sending a strong message, while the relationships between management and these workers were not strong enough for them to open up. The Portuguese Silva and his management team, however, clearly expected a different collaboration within the company. They had counted on individuals:

> *As a Country Director, I had been relying on the initiative of individuals. Obviously, I had counted on the foremen to play the go-between and to report important issues to me or to one of my managers. And I had also assumed that one of our Angolan frontliners who had received an extensive training in Portugal, for instance, would have done so. I remember very well how he had received a gift from our Portuguese CEO just before returning to Angola and I had assumed this would also have stimulated him to talk to me, or to inform me when there was trouble ahead.*

Besides the difference on collectivism/individualism, the difference in power distance was most probably also at play here. Generally speaking, a high-power distance culture demands a lot from leaders and managers, and Silva had not been fully aware of it. Countless businessmen from lower PDI cultures think it is easy to be a leader in a high PDI society: they assume that subordinates do as they are told, and no questions asked. However, this notion is false. Being (what is considered) a good leader in a large power distance context can be quite hard work. There are several reasons for this. One is that the relationship between leader and subordinate is generally far more personal than the contract-based relationship in a society like the USA, for instance. People tend to be loyal to a leader and follow instructions, but at the same time they expect genuine concern and care in return. A comparative study about African and western values on motivation, for instance, carried out by Iguisi in 1994 in Nigeria, revealed that "affectionate relationships between superior and subordinate motivated them much more than recognized achievement, challenging work, and participation in decision-making."[58] This demands investment

[58] Iguisi (1994, 2014, p. 63).

of time and energy from leadership, and it often demands different rules and more flexibility within the HR department than in Western-style companies.

Another reason for the demand put on leadership in a high PDI society is the fact that the flow of information needs special and continuous attention. This is at the core of the problem that was detected after the culture shock experienced by Silva: his company was far more vulnerable than he thought it was and there seemed to be a serious issue concerning the information flow from bottom-up to the top and back. In a society with a relatively small power distance, equality is highly valued, and people feel they have the right to speak up and tell their boss in case there is an issue or in case they think that a certain decision will not be effective. In a large power distance culture, like Angola, as was mentioned, subordinates often display high respect for their leader(s); they assume that they probably don't have all the information leadership has at its disposal, and therefore, they are not in the position to disagree (at least not publicly) or to take the initiative when projects run into trouble. This is reinforced in conjunction with the collectivist tendency to preserve group harmony, which leads to indirect communication styles and avoidance of confrontation in speech.

At the same time, it is only natural that leaders all over the world need all the information they can get to take the best decisions. Hence local leaders in large power distance cultures, mostly unconsciously, consider it their responsibility and never-ending task to go out of their way to seek information. They may make themselves seen at the workplace, asking people how they are doing and making themselves available for a junior manager or employee to hint or say a few words in private. They may do far more checking and verification; they may have informal informants (possibly from the same collectivist in-group) and find all kinds of creative ways to receive news on progress or setbacks. While a manager in low PDI context may sit at his/her desk and considers no news to be good news, a manager in the high PDI context is more often actively going out to listen, check, control, and inspect.

After this analysis, I realized that indeed we had not done enough to seek information ourselves, as a management team. We expected trouble, disagreement, or information about mistakes we made, to reach us automatically, or through certain individuals. We hadn't built enough (personal) relationships and trust with our front liners and to them, we now understood, we didn't show ourselves enough at the workplace. The fact that most of our frontline workers were working at different sites throughout the city and even further inside the country aggravated this issue.

It's been stated that a third dimension, the avoidance of certainty, calls for phenomena that create clarity and take ambiguity away, such as rules, regulations, structure, and/or formalization. For the sake of analysis, the different dimensions have been mentioned separately so far, but in reality, these basic values play invisible and intertwined roles simultaneously in daily operations. Wursten called the countries with the combination of large power distance, collectivism, and a relatively high uncertainty avoidance, the Pyramid culture cluster: hierarchical, rather formal and structured, with more people at the bottom, few people above and one person on top.[59] Every person in the pyramid has its own position and role to play and acts responsibly as a dignified member of the whole community.[60] While describing the Pyramid countries Wursten observes that "there is a strong need to formalize communication between the various levels within the organization and there is need to formalize the relation between colleagues."[61] While discussing PDI in the previous paragraph, it has been observed already, that in 'traditional' structures in sub-Saharan Africa, voicing opinion may have been formalized or ritualized: designated spaces, like specific family gatherings, village councils, or courts, created to speak up and to participate. As it turns out, within the company of Silva, this specific space to open up, to voice opinion and communicate suggestions, and also possibly to create relationships and to forge community, seemed to be lacking.

Wursten describes more features of a typical Pyramid organization: "Pyramid structures have a strong need for centralization. (…) Directive is always from the top to the lower levels. The lower levels are only supposed to implement what the official directive allows them to do, but nothing more. Unforeseen events are escalated into the hierarchical system."[62] Hence, he talks about top-down mandating[63] and in case of an issue, people would have to go back to a hierarchical level above, in order to ask for further instructions.

[59] Wursten (2019).

[60] See Dandala on manhood (2009, pp. 269–270).

[61] Wursten (1997, p. 18).

[62] Wursten (2019, p. 57).

[63] Wursten (2019, p. 85).

Big accidents are known for having many causes, and this is also true for the strike. Apart from the lacking space and trusted relationships for information sharing and dialogue, for once, the mandate had been wrong. After their complaint, the message to the frontliners was that the renumeration for the weekend-extra time had been correctly calculated, which was not true and probably caused anger. Fourthly, the personal leadership competencies of the people at the core of the incident left room for improvement. Generally, it calls for a fair amount of leadership competence to strike the balance between clear (and sometimes harsh) instructions on the one hand and offering a listening ear on the other. As a result, no one went back up into the hierarchical system to ask for new instructions; it simply didn't occur. Also, the choice between loyalty and responsibility towards a (rather unknown) company-mission, on the one hand, or towards team members on the other, asked for a careful balancing act, which, in this case, didn't fall into the favour of the company.

As mentioned, on that faithful Saturday, Silva did actually talk to two of the people involved. However, it was only at surface level, they mentioned they didn't know what was going on and they didn't provide any information which could help solve the situation. It is this silence, together with the fact that afterwards these people also didn't have anything to say for themselves, which baffled Silva the most. Lanzer, coming from a high PDI country himself, explains: "In high PDI cultures (...) one often finds that mistakes and 'bad news' are hidden from the boss' view, for subordinates fear a negative reaction. It's the old story of 'shooting the messenger'. Nobody wants to play the role of being the bearer of bad news, so bad performance and mistakes are hidden from the boss."[64] Therefore, the reaction of the individuals Silva spoke to may not have been in the best interest of the company, yet it was culturally explainable. Thus executed, they did not betray team members, nor had they bypassed the hierarchy, and at face level, they made themselves available over the phone to their Country Director. One person might have been in the position to reach out to management earlier, but probably didn't feel well enough connected; another one might have felt closely related, but not at all in the right position to bypass several hierarchical layers.

[64] Lanzer (2017, p. 37).

The workers, as a group, reacted completely according to their cultural traits. They must have felt hurt by the lack of a listening ear. On top, they had worked their way up two levels within the pyramid, and without strong relationships nor a formalized space to communicate, moving up another layer was probably considered a bridge too far.

It is this combination, the cultural differences on power distance, collectivism, and uncertainty avoidance, combined with a wrong mandate and poor leadership capabilities of key individuals, that has probably accounted most for the situation in which the company found itself during the wild strike. Continuing the cultural search heightens the risk of forcing reality into the 6-D model. With this risk in mind though, it is possible to point at two more dimensions, which are at least not contradictory with the events. Firstly, the short-term orientation of Angolan culture portrays a relatively principled people. The frontline workers were at that stage not willing to endure the situation any longer, they did not want to wait for another chance to put the issue on the agenda. Nor did they feel part or parcel of the long-term vision of the company, so they decided to stand up for the principle of fair pay for their extra-time hours immediately: here and now.

Secondly, we find a relatively high score for Angola on the dimension of indulgence. Leisure time is generally considered important in high IVR countries. At the same time, work was frequently done during the weekends and the workers were quite eager to work these extra-time hours due to the financial remuneration. Now that this extra remuneration was at stake and the way to solve it seemed blocked, it was logical for them to choose for leisure over the weekend and show up for work on Monday.

In conclusion of the etic research, I may say that I had been bewildered right after the strike. Although I still do not agree with the decisions taken by some of my employees, applying the dimensions of Hofstede to our situation has made the events look far more logical and understandable. It was a combination of causes from the workers point of view and there were certain flaws in the organization which did not prove to have enough resolving power. All in all, we had built a system that did not fit very well in the surrounding cultural environment. We would certainly take these insights along in our organizational change process.

References

Ailon, G. (2008). Mirror, mirror on the wall: Culture's consequences in a value test of its own design. *Academy of Management Review, 33*, 885–904.

Ball, D. A., McCulloch, Jr., W. H., Frantz, P. L., Geringer, J. M., & Minor, M. S. (2004). *International business: The challenges of global competition* (9th ed.). McGraw-Hill Irwin.

Beugelsdijk, S., Maseland, R., & van Hoorn, A. (2015). Are scores on Hofstede's dimensions of national culture stable over time? A cohort analysis. In *Global Strategy Journal, 5*, 223–240.

Beugelsdijk, S., & Welzel, C. (2018). Dimensions and dynamics of national culture: Synthesizing Hofstede with Inglehart. *Journal of Cross-Cultural Psychology, 49*(10), 1469–1505.

Boubakri, N., Guedhami, O., Kwok, C. C. Y., & Safar, W. (2016). National culture and privatization: The relationship between collectivism and residual state ownership. *Journal of International Business Studies, 47*, 170–190.

Chinese Culture Connection. (1987). Chinese values and the search for culture-free dimensions of culture. *Journal of Cross-Cult: Psychology, 18*(2), 143–164.

Dandala, M. (2009). Cows never die: Embracing African cosmology in the process of economic growth. In M. F. Murove (Ed.), *African ethics: An anthology of comparative and applied ethics* (pp. 259–277). KwaZulu-Natal Press.

Drogendijk, R., & Slangen, A. (2006). Hofstede, Schwartz, or managerial perceptions? The effects of different cultural distance measures on establishment mode choices by multinational enterprises. *International Business Review, 15*, 361–380.

Finuras, P. (2013). *Cultural values and trust in institutions: A comparative study between Portugal, Angola, Cape Verde Islands and Mozambique* (Doctoral Research). Luso University Lisbon.

Fischer, R., Vauclair, M. C., Fontaine, J. R. J., & Schwartz, S. H. (2010). Are individual-level and country-level value structures different? Testing Hofstede's legacy with the Schwartz value survey. *Journal of Cross-Cultural Psychology, 41*(2), 135–151.

Graness, A. (2016). Writing the history of philosophy in Africa: Where to begin? *Journal of African Cultural Studies, 28*(2), 132–146. https://doi.org/10.1080/13696815.2015.1053799

Gyekye, K. (1997). *Tradition and modernity: Philosophical reflections on the African experience*. Oxford University Press.

Gyekye, K. (2004). *The unexamined life: Philosophy and the African experience.* Sankofa Publishing Company.

Hall, E., & Reed Hall, M. (1990). *Understanding cultural differences.* Intercultural Press.

Hofstede, G. (1980a). *Culture's consequences: International differences in work-related values.* Sage.

Hofstede, G. (1980b). Motivation, leadership, and organization: Do American theories apply abroad? *Organizational Dynamics, 9*, 42–63.

Hofstede, G. (1998). *Masculinity and femininity: The taboo dimensions of national cultures*. Sage.

Hofstede, G. (2001). *Culture's consequences: Comparing values, behaviors, institutions and organizations across nations* (2nd ed.). Sage.

Hofstede, G. (2002). Dimensions do not exist: A reply to Brendan McSweeney. *Human Relations, 55*(11), 1355–1361.

Hofstede, G., Hofstede, G. J., & Minkov, M. (2010). *Cultures and organizations: Software of the mind*. McGraw-Hill.

Hofstede, G. J. (2019). *BOSS Blog 1: Do cultures change?* https://geerthofstede.com/boss-blog-1-do-cultures-change/. Consulted on 12 August 2020.

Holtbrügge, D. (2022). *Intercultural management: Concepts, practice, critical reflection*. Sage.

House, R. J., Hanges, P. J., Javidan, M., Dorfman, P. W., & Gupta, V. (2004). *Culture, leadership, and organizations: The GLOBE study of 62 societies*. Sage.

Iguisi, O. (1994). Appropriate management in an African culture. *Journal of Management in Nigeria, 30*(1), 16–24.

Iguisi, O. (2014). African values for the practice of HRM. *Beykent University Journal of Social Sciences, 7*(1), 56–77.

Inglehart, R., & Baker, W. E. (2000). Modernization, cultural change, and the persistence of traditional values. *American Sociological Review, 65*(1), 19–51.

Kirkman, B. L., Lowe, K. B., & Gibson, C. B. (2006). A quarter century of 'culture's consequences': A review of empirical research incorporating Hofstede's cultural values framework. *Journal of International Business Studies, 37*, 285–320.

Kirkman, B. L., Lowe, K. B., & Gibson, C. B. (2017). *A retrospective on cultures consequences: The 35-year journey*. https://api.research-repository.uwa.edu.au/ws/portalfiles/portal/24299027/Kirkman_et._al._2017_A_retrospective_on_Culture_s_Consequences.pdf. Consulted on 30 December 2022.

Kluckhohn, F. R., & Strodtbeck, F. I. (1961). *Variations in value orientation*. Evanston University Press.

Kwek, D. (2003). Decolonizing and re-presenting culture's consequences: A postcolonial critique of cross-cultural studies in management. In A. Prasad (Ed.), *Postcolonial theory and organizational analysis* (pp. 121–148). Palgrave Macmillan.

Lanzer, F. (2017). *Leading across cultures in practice*. LCO Partners BV.

Mbigi, L. (2005). *The spirit of African leadership*. Knowledge Resources.

Mbiti, J. S. (1969). *African religions & philosophy*. Heinemann.

McSweeney, B. (2002). Hofstede's model of national cultural differences and their consequences: A triumph of faith—A failure of analysis. *Human Relations, 55*, 89–118.

Menkiti, I. A. (1984). African philosophy: An introduction. In R. A. Wright (Ed.), *Person and community in African traditional thought* (pp. 171–181). University Press of America.

Menkiti, I. A. (2006). On the normative conception of a person. In K. Wiredu (Ed.), *A companion to African philosophy* (pp. 324–331). Blackwell.

Metz, T. (2022). *A relational moral theory: African ethics in and beyond the continent*. Oxford University Press.

Meyer, E. (2014). *The culture map*. Public Affairs.

Minkov, M. (2007). *What makes us different and similar: A new interpretation of the world values survey and other cross-cultural data*. Klasika i Stil.

Minkov, M. (2014). *Cross-cultural analysis: The science and art of comparing the world's modern societies and their cultures*. Sage.

Minkov, M. (2018). A revision of Hofstede's model of national culture: Old evidence and new data from 56 countries. *Cross Cultural & Strategic Management, 25*(2), 231–256.

Minkov, M., & Kaasa, A. (2022). Do dimensions of culture exist objectively? A validation of the revised Minkov-Hofstede model of culture with world values survey items and scores for 102 countries. *Journal of International Management, 28*(4), 100791.

Minkov, M., Vignoles, V. L., Welzel, C., Akaliyski, P., Bond, M. H., Kaasa, A., & Smith, P. B. (2023, forthcoming). *Comparative culturology and cross-cultural psychology: How comparing societal cultures differs from comparing the minds of individuals across cultures*. See: https://www.youtube.com/watch?v=r74JmVwnmoM. Consulted on 27 October 2023.

Müller, L. (2023). Human wellbeing in intercultural philosophical perspective: A focus on the Akan philosophy of Wiredu, Gyekye, and Appiah. In B. Bateye, M. Masaeli, L. Müller, & A. Roothaan (Eds.), *Well-being in African philosophy: Insights for a global ethics of development* (pp. 13–49). Lexington Books by Rowman & Littlefield.

Noorderhaven, N.G. & Tidjani, B. (2001). Culture, Governance, and Economic Performance: An Explorative Study with a special focus on Africa. *International Journal of Cross Cultural Management 1*(1): 31-52.

Van Pinxteren, B. (2018). *African identities: A new perspective*. African Studies Centre.

Reiter, B. (2021). The African origins of democracy. *Academia Letters*, Article 414. https://doi.org/10.20935/AL414

Schneider, S., Barsoux, J. L., & Stahl, G. K. (2014). *Managing across cultures* (3rd ed.). Pearson Education Limited.

Schwartz, S. H. (1994). Beyond individualism/collectivism: New cultural dimensions of values. In U. Kim, C. Kagitcibasi, H. C. Triandis, S. C. Choi, & G. Yoon (Eds.), *Individualism/collectivism: Theory, method and application* (pp. 85–119). Sage.

Schwartz, S. H. (2006). A theory of cultural value orientations: Explication and applications. *Comparative Sociology, 5*(2–3), 137–182.
Schwartz, S. H. (2011). Studying values: Personal adventure, future directions. *Journal of Cross-Cultural Psychology, 42*(2), 307–319.
Smelser, N. J. (1992). Culture: Coherent or incoherent. In R. Munch & N. J. Smelser (Eds.), *Theory of culture*. University of California Press. http://ark.cdlib.org/ark:/13030/ft8q2nb667/
Smit, I., & Siegmund, W. (2014). *An engineer's Odyssey*. Siegmund audiovisuele produkties. https://www.youtube.com/watch?v=xbLjgm-9Pkw. Consulted 27 August 2023.
Smith, P. B., Dugan, D., & Trompenaars, F. (1996). National culture and the values of organizational employees: A dimensional analysis across 43 nations. *Journal of Cross-Cultural Psychology, 27*(2), 231–264.
Smith, P. B., Trompenaars, F., & Dugan, S. (1995). The rotter locus of control scale in 43 countries: A test of cultural relativity. *International Journal of Psychology, 30*(3), 377–400.
Smith, P. B., & Bond, M. H. (1999). *Social psychology across cultures* (2nd ed.). Allyn & Bacon.
Taras, V., Steel, P., & Kirkman, B. L. (2012). Improving national cultural indices using a longitudinal meta-analysis of Hofstede's dimensions. *Journal World Business, 47*(3), 329–341.
Triandis, H. C. (1982). Review of culture's consequences: International differences in work-related values. *Human Organization, 41*(1), 86–90.
Trompenaars, F. (1993). *Riding the waves of culture*. Economist Books.
Venkateswaran, R. T., & Ojha, A. K. (2019). Abandon Hofstede-based research? Not yet! A perspective from the philosophy of the social sciences. *Asia Pacific Business Review, 25*(3), 413–434. https://doi.org/10.1080/13602381.2019.1584487
Williamson, D. (2002). Forward from a critique of Hofstede's model of national culture. *Human Relations, 55*(11), 1373–1395.
Wiredu, K. (2008). Social philosophy in postcolonial Africa: Some preliminaries concerning communalism and communitarianism. *South African Journal of Philosophy, 27*(4), 332–339.
Wiredu, K. (2009). An oral philosophy of personhood: Comments on philosophy and orality. *Research in African Literatures, 40*(1), 8–18.
Wursten, H. (1997). Mental images the influence of culture on (economic) policy. In *Report of the international colloquium on regional governance and sustainable development*. United Nations Publication ST/ESA/PAD/SER. E, 46.
Wursten, H. (2019). *The 7 mental images of national culture: Leading and managing in a globalized world*. Helsinki.

CHAPTER 5

Genchi Genbutsu of the Toyota Way: Finding Local Perspectives

Abstract For the emic approach an adaptation of Toyota innovation philosophy, named *Genchi Genbutsu*, is being applied. In English, this practice is usually translated as a directive to 'go and see for yourself.' For the company it involved formulating questions, interviewing employees, having open conversations with other local inhabitants and validation with local business leaders. Sound explanations and experiences are being described, about local wisdom, customs, values, and beliefs, which inspired management to develop a culture-specific intervention. The chapter ends with the formulation of a small list of Angolan cultural elements that were found in the research, which would guide the change process. Featuring in this list are the respect for authority; the collectivist values; the continuous representative role people in Angola take; the use of familiar yet rather formal committee structures. Last but not least a form of leadership was found and explained, in the form of the Soba, or Angolan chief.

Keywords Emic cultural research · Genchi Genbutsu · Soba · Representative role · Angolan Chief · Toyota way

A. Vonk and V. F. Silva, *Cultural Confluence in Organizational Change*, Palgrave Studies in African Leadership,
https://doi.org/10.1007/978-3-031-45403-5_5

In the past chapter, the comparison between Angolan and Portuguese cultures on a few dimensions was presented, and how these differences may have impacted the situation of the company and the strike. This chapter will delve deeper into the emic way of studying culture. How do the people in Angola themselves describe their culture, beliefs, and norms in the workplace? Is it possible to apply the cultural dimensions one step further: how do they actually find form in this particular context (in the more outer layers of the onion)? Even more specifically, Silva was on the lookout for local concepts that he, together with his workers, may use within their company.

An Application of the Toyota Way

The approach that Silva used to delve deeper into the authentic knowledge of his surroundings in Angola is called *Genchi Genbutsu*. It is one of the 14 principles of management of the successful Toyota company, described in 'The Toyota Way.'[1] In English, it is translated as a directive: 'Go and see for yourself' and the goal is to gain a deep understanding by observation and close listening. Any form of problem solving, according to this philosophy, should be based on deep first-hand knowledge obtained on-site and in-person. This management principle assumes that it is unacceptable to take anything for granted or to rely only on the reports from others. When Liker asked Toyota employees what distinguishes the Toyota Way from other management approaches, the most common response was *Genchi Genbutsu*—whether he was interviewing staff from manufacturing, product development, sales, distribution, or public affairs. In other words, it was applied in many different departments.

There's an interesting and clarifying story of a very successful product design for the Toyota Sienna Mini, based on the *Genchi Genbutsu* philosophy. To figure out how to improve the minivan model, Yuji Yokoya proposed a road trip of more than 85.000 kilometres driving across the USA, Canada, and Mexico. It led to the development of extra features and appeal of the van, boosting the Sienna's sales with 60% in the following year.

[1] Liker (2004).

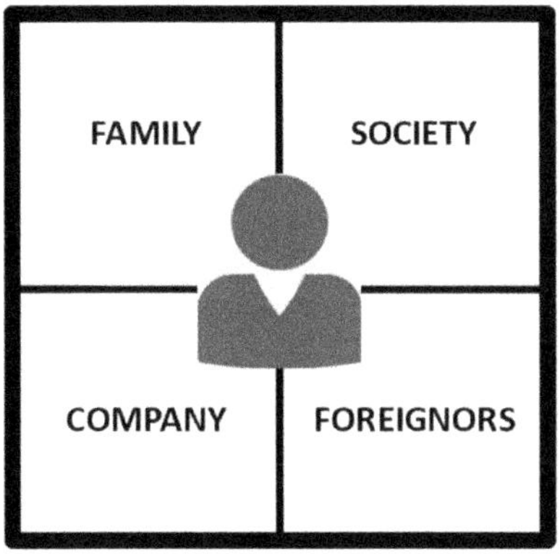

Fig. 5.1 Four main areas of interest for emic research

Silva used this philosophy to develop a methodology for the generation of local knowledge, norms, and customs. In order to structure their search, the management team decided to divide their quest for local features into four main areas of day-to-day life: Family, Society, Company, and Foreigners (Fig. 5.1).

Based on his experience in Angola, on his readings of Hofstede, and stimulated by true curiosity to find out Angolan perspectives and organizational principles, Vasco, together with his management team, formulated several thought-provoking questions for all four areas, to receive and develop further insight. For instance, some of the questions, they set out with, were the following:

Family

- How is informal authority distributed inside a family?
- Who do you consider being your family?
- What responsibilities do you have inside your family?
- If there is any problem among families, how it is solved?

Society

- Are there ethnic groups in society and how do they relate to each other?
- How are traditional authorities in society organized; what are their roots?

- What are the main difficulties that you face when coming to work?
- Do you perceive the national society as fair?

Foreigners

- Do you feel that foreigners are well received by nationals?
- What are the three aspects that you appreciate or dislike most in a foreigner that comes to work in your country?
- Do you think foreigners integrate easily in society or remain in strict groups?
- If there is a conflict with a foreigner, how do you address it?

Company

- Do you think the international company's management and leadership styles are adapted to the local workforce?
- Do you prefer working with national managers or foreign managers?
- What are the responsibilities of the company and the employees towards each other?
- How do you define the relationship among national peers within the company?

We posed these questions to ourselves within the management team, to business leaders, both Angolan and expats, and to our employees. As a Country Director I also had some very interesting and long conversations with the mothers of some of my befriended Angolan business leaders. Most of our employees and frontline workers were quite young and, as is the case in most of Africa, the youth finds it hard to discuss local custom freely (especially with their Portuguese boss). They do not consider themselves fit to talk about these things. The mothers, on the other hand, were natural speakers and this created a lot of clarity.

Apart from these conversations and deep listening exercises, Silva also took time to pose himself these and similar questions after any interaction or observation that occurred.

This way the technique created some sort of a mental speed bump for me, stimulating me to sit down and reflect. We received all kinds of answers about the most important behaviours, norms, values, and structures, and we needed to stop, evaluate and (re) interpret continuously, in an ongoing creative process. In this interpretation stage, we did our best to postpone all judgements and to maintain a non-prejudicial perception and evaluation of information, while integrating information from several sources.

With the answers and insights from outside sources at hand, I was more apt to have the conversations, mostly one-on-one, with frontline workers and other employees as well. My veritable interest and increasing knowledge did give some of our workers confidence and stimulated their thinking about undisclosed fields and the underlying assumptions of their own culture. We travelled the country, visited our different sites and office in the south. Slowly but steadily we received a much broader view of the culture we were a part of and the values that were cherished here.

When exploiting this tool, Silva and his team learned that not every cultural insight generated proved to be useful in the end. It was just fine to accept a certain interpretation or insight, leave it to rest for a moment, and explore further to find more. In the process certain insights gained momentum, while others simply moved to the background.

Furthermore, they also found that the true value of the tool is oftentimes found in the areas one is focusing on and the questions being asked: what you ask is what you find. The four areas studied, and the questions posed in this case, were selected based on the team's experience specifically for Angola, and it is possible to pivot both for other countries.

All in all, the tool itself and adapting it to the four areas of inquiry made us leap forward and we can advise all leaders: next time you may be stuck in stereotypical assumptions and/or there does not seem to be anything you can do to understand a specific behaviour in a different culture, pull out the "go, ask and interpret" tool and find the right cultural answers.

Local Cultural Insights Results

The period of observation, posing questions, having all kinds of conversations, going back and forth, and generating knowledge and insight, lasted several weeks. In this paragraph, there is a selection of the observations of Silva and his management team, which made it possible for them to connect the dots. The questions in the previous paragraph were very useful to guide their thinking and prevent missing important information, but they did not answer each question one by one.

Family

We came to understand much better how the collectivistic nature of Angolan society works out in practice and we started to appreciate the authentic culture of group solidarity and interdependence even more, paramount for the survival of all members of a community. For instance, children only rarely become orphans, despite the very low life expectancy for adult parents. The reason is that the roles of mother and father are, by definition, not vested in a single individual with respect to a single child. I remember particularly the broad meaning of the words mother and brother, which is very often used for aunts and cousins, respectively. In the Angolan society, all aunts are called mothers and the word aunt is hardly ever used. I also recalled several situations in which employees had been asking jobs for their brothers, only for us to find out later that the candidates were cousins or even second grade relatives.

Suddenly we also understood the popular greeting "Estamos Juntos" (in English: We are together) much better. It is used frequently as a goodbye by Angolans. Emphasizing this togetherness as a greeting when people part points out that the relationship remains intact, even when the other is out of sight. Moreover, it expresses the notion that people actually 'do take the other person along,' even when they part.

Completely in line with this and an insight which struck us deeply, is that it is very common that each individual actually represents not only him/herself, but rather represents the whole family. Individual identity seems to be replaced by a representative role. The individual is like a stand-in for the group to which he/she belongs, effectively and at all times. The individual identity is replaced with a larger societal identity, which is vested within each person: everybody feels part of the 'we' at every given moment (whether the others are physically present or not). Thus, the families are reflected in the individual and this phenomenon is extended to villages, districts, provinces, and regions. This representative role places high demands on the individual to behave in the highest standards and to portray the highest possible virtues that society strives for. After all, if one is making a mistake, the outer world perceives it as a mistake of the whole group, and no one would want to be responsible for this.

Society

The team also posed questions on the way society was led in Angola. They were informed that they were ruled by a traditional authority called Soba, which acts in a certain community, named the Sobado or Quimbo. The Soba knows all his Sobado inhabitants personally. He takes decisions regarding inhabitant's disputes and litigations (land, money, agriculture and livestock, water, relationships, etc.); prevents the development of problems inside the community (diseases, conflict, witchcraft, sorcery, etc.); and he organizes special events in the village (end of girl and boy puberty, marriages, holy days, etc.). The Soba authority focuses mainly on the moral aspects of human behaviour, acting as a tribal leader that plays the role of judge without a court, police without a squad, or mayor without a city hall. Additionally, the Soba acts as the community representative when the Sobado needs to communicate with government authorities, providing very valuable information regarding particular society problems, such as disputes, disease, death, or other issues. The Soba is also responsible for the security of the community and establishes the rules that should be followed by the community inhabitants.

If the Soba is unable to solve any particular issue and needs some advice, Silva's informants continued, he makes a written report to the Big Soba that discusses the problem in a Soba Committee and this organ gives advice to the individual Soba. The Big Soba acts as the leader of a group of Sobas of a certain region. Usually, in terms of succession, the Soba successor is selected by the Soba Committee. However, in some Angola regions, the new Soba is chosen to be the nephew of the previous one, son of one of his sisters (in a matrilineal fashion).

According to my informants, the Soba is selected by his high behavioural standards, genuine good character and intelligence, sense of justice and equal rights, great leadership and communication qualities, good decision-making skills and, above all, wisdom acquired with age.

In the institution of the Soba, we recognized the difference in power distance between Angola and Portugal and the community acceptance of unequal distribution of power. The Soba is accepted to acquire a lot of power over longer periods of time (and probably until death). To us it felt contradictory at times: while people seem close to each other in terms of group solidarity, they appear distant and more formal when it comes to power differences. During the conversations with our employees, however, we observed that this wasn't contradictory to them at all. We also noticed that the institutions like the Soba, the Soba Committee, and also the criteria by which the Soba was described truly inspired them. In the end, therefore, these institutions proved to be very useful in our company context.

Foreign Corporations

The questions concerning the foreigner's acceptance that Silva and his team posed were answered very positively. The respondents made it clear that foreigners (like Silva himself) are very welcome to the country. Generally, Angolan workers expressed their happiness to work for foreign companies. They even said they have more confidence in foreign managers and their management practices because they expect foreign managers to act more professional than their own compatriots. The team understood that many workers look at Angolan managers with some level of suspicion, expecting them to enrich themselves rather than taking the right decisions for the company.

It is the question whether these answers tell the complete story. Åkesson, during her interviews with Angolan respondents in Luanda, detected some other sentiments as well:

> "As one young Angolan student said, when I asked him why he and others were afraid of talking about their perceptions of the Portuguese: "The Portuguese have support from highly placed politicians and from generals". (...) Others saw 'the Portuguese' in themselves as a threatening and growing power, especially in their capacity of employers. Fear run deepest among unskilled Angolans working on insecure contracts in Portuguese companies or under Portuguese managers or both, but also Angolans in more stable positions were afraid of losing their jobs if they criticised Portuguese superiors."[2]

Silva and his team did find that many local workers would like to see changes in the managing style of foreign managers, including leadership, decision-making, communication, and teamwork: they feel that the foreign managers maintain too much distance. On top, most nationals believe that multinational corporations don't have policies of management adaptation to the culture of the country. However, the workers

[2] Åkesson (2018, p. 28).

found it very hard to identify or formulate any intervention towards an improvement into the right direction.

One other finding in this respect was that in terms of conflict resolution with foreigners or corporations, nationals seem to avoid any means of confrontation and most people in Angola believe that in case you are not happy in your job with a foreign company, the best solution is to leave. This is in line with the feature of a collectivist culture in terms of conflict avoidance and the need to maintain harmony.

Only in hindsight did we realize that this is what happened to one the two people at the centre (in between management and workers) during the strike. They were not dismissed at the time, but it remains true that from my more individualistic and lower PDI point of view, I had felt a serious breach in trust. There is no doubt in my mind that they must have noticed this. I had expected them to speak up, both before the strike (to warn us) but also after the strike (to explain themselves). In the course of the year that followed the strike, one of them left the company rather silently.

Organization

Finally, the team gained more insights into the local forms of organization.

We disclosed that families and communities usually meet in committees to find consensus, to solve problems and disputes and other issues among themselves. The higher authority roles inside a family and, consequently in a certain committee structure, are granted to elder males and maternal uncles.

It was especially during the observation of a ceremony that this insight fully made sense to Silva. As mentioned, apart from asking questions to find answers, the tool of *Genchi Genbutsu* is also used to observe very closely. While describing the Toyota Way, Liker mentions that he often heard a story about Fuji Cho, the first president of the Toyota plant in Georgetown, Kentucky. Cho would visit the factory floor in the morning, stand still, and stare. People would greet him, but he would not respond and continue to stand and stare, "as if off into space." After quite some time Cho would relax and, as if he realized at that point that he was not alone, he would greet with a smile.[3] This close observation method can

[3] Liker (2004, p. 223).

also be used for deep cultural understanding outside the company. Some of the concepts that the company used to formulate their organizational change after the research can, therefore, be found within the following experience.

I was fortunate to be present at a traditional Angolan wedding ceremony, in which I got valuable insight regarding the consensus oriented and communal society. All around Africa, traditional weddings are special celebrations of the natural continuity of families and communities, I was told. In all these communities, the bride plays a very special role and is treated with maximum respect because she is a link between the ancestors and the unborn and in that sense considered the most important part of the family.

It all starts with an event called 'knocking the doors' to the bride's house. The name comes from the fact that every visitor must knock on the door of a house, before entering and receiving hospitality. In this 'knocking the doors' ceremony, the future husband, together with his father, brothers, and some elder uncles, set off to the bride's house with the objective to announce their intentions for establishing the relationship. For this ceremony, the family members of the fiancé bring along liquor, beer, and soda, to present to his future bride's family.

According to protocol, while presenting the drinks, the father or elder uncle of the fiancé requests the bride's family whether they can enter the property to formally make their appeal. If the drinks are accepted, it means permission has been granted to the visitors to state their intentions. The two families meet in a formal manner, as if they are having a committee meeting, in order to find agreement regarding the wedding. Most of the time, this ceremony is carried out three or four weeks ahead of the traditional marriage ceremony. The meeting is finalized by finding consensus on the specific date for the traditional wedding ceremony.

Approximately one week after the 'knocking the doors' event, the bride's family presents a dowry list of items that the family of the fiancé should bring to the traditional wedding ceremony, listing items such as: suit for the bride's father, dress for the bride's mother, typical African textiles for the bride's aunts, men scarf, shoes, wine, liquor, soda, beer and money. The money is destined, and should be enough, to buy items for the bride layette to start marital life with her new husband, such as cooking pans, domestic LPG cylinder, linen, cutlery, plates, and a stove.

For the scheduled date, the groom and his family, in conjunction with invited guests, show up early at the house of the family of the bride. At first, the family of the groom sits on one side, while the bride's family sits on the reverse side: the two families facing each other. While the bride is not present, the family of the groom will start by presenting the dowry items on the list, one by one. Each item is checked exhaustively to be sure everything asked on the list is being presented. During these proceedings, the groom rarely speaks, as all the actual speaking and negotiation is conducted on his behalf by the designated spokesperson of his family, usually his elder uncle or brother. If all items are accepted and the families find agreement to proceed with the traditional ceremony, the bride is asked to come to the room and the groom offers and fits the engagement ring to the bride. These proceedings are then followed by a traditional dinner and party between both family members and guests. The religious or civil wedding ceremonies are usually organized the day or week after.

While I was witnessing these proceedings, I reached completely new levels of understanding into attitude and culturally correct conduct, often only accessible through experience. It was at moments like these that I observed the consensus-driven behaviour in familiar, yet rather formal committee structures; the representative roles that people play in various situations; the balance between speaking up and respect for the elderly; and the importance of time bound traditions. In fact, for me it was one of those thrilling moments in which I had the feeling I actually understood part of the Angolan psyche. Slowly but steadily, the whole puzzle started to fall into place.

Building Blocks

After the analysis as described in this and in the previous chapter, the team sieved out the most important elements which could guide them further. These form the building blocks to be used for the transformation to take place. The team was looking for simple, genuine, and logical local concepts and the following phenomena stood out for them:

- the communal spirit, based on collectivist principles.
- the role of representing the community, vested in each individual and encouraging responsible behaviour.
- the necessity for a leader to seek information and to go out and check, control, and inspect while simultaneously taking care of the subordinates.
- the personal relationships between the leader and his subordinates, facilitating a good information flow within communities.

- the harmonious, consensus-driven communication in familiar, yet at the same time rather formal spaces and committee structures.
- the acceptance of local leadership of the Soba, that was defined in very well prescribed terms, and which portrayed high levels of behaviour and integrity.

Our next challenge was to develop a culture-specific intervention, to integrate these concepts into an organizational change process, with the ultimate goal to glue the whole company together and transforming it into a culture-centred workplace, in a lasting way.

References

Åkesson, L. (2018). *Postcolonial Portuguese migration to Angola*. Palgrave Macmillan.

Liker, K. J. (2004). *The Toyota way: 14 management principles from the world's greatest manufacturer*. McGraw-Hill.

PART III

Organizational Change

After the extensive cultural analysis described in the previous chapters, we had become inspired as a management team by the cultural insights we had gained about indigenous African values and institutions. Our next challenge was to find the correct key: how could we authentically connect and merge with the wealth of institutions and norms that we found? how could we bridge the gaps between the traditional and modern aspects of African life, on the one hand, and between the African and Portuguese side, on the other? How to fit our value systems together, for us to become one, as a company, sharing information and collaborating closely for the good of all?

In this Part III, the organizational, transformational change that took place within the subsidiary will be described. This part is the most practical part of the book, and the descriptions will come primarily from Silva himself, supplemented with observations from Vonk and with citations from some of the frontliners involved. Chapter 6 describes the design and practical steps and activities undertaken, while Chapter 7 describes the results, the effects of the new situation, what did it bring about and how was it evaluated overall?

CHAPTER 6

The Process of Organizational Design to Bridge the Culture Gap

Abstract Part III describes the organizational change that was adopted. Using the elements of the research, the company was able to combine the best of both worlds and created a new Council, as an innovative organ within the company structure, enabling the involvement of frontline workers and bridging the gap with management. This chapter provides the design: the set-up; the expectations of management; the selection of members; the first meeting and naming the council; the organization and formulation of mission and values; and finally the activities that were planned. The Council was officially called the Culture Council while informally the name Soba Council remained in vogue.

Keywords Organizational design · Culture Council · Works Council · Soba Council · Internal information flow

Finding a Key

As concluded from the analysis in part II, there were several elements of findings which became the building blocks. The communal spirit clearly stood out, based on collectivist principles and the attached role

A. Vonk and V. F. Silva, *Cultural Confluence in Organizational Change*, Palgrave Studies in African Leadership,
https://doi.org/10.1007/978-3-031-45403-5_6

of each member to represent the community in a dignified and responsible manner. The importance of personal relationships between the leader and his subordinates had become apparent, facilitating a good information flow within communities. It included the necessity for a leader to seek information and to go out and check, control, and inspect while simultaneously taking care of the subordinates, acting like 'a benevolent father' (or mother). Also, the harmonious, consensus-driven behaviour stood out, in familiar, yet at the same time rather formal (ritualized) spaces and committee structures. Finally, the conversations within the management team as well as with the frontliners had indicated enthusiasm for the local leadership of the Soba, that was defined in very well prescribed terms, and which portrayed high levels of behaviour and integrity.

It was a leap of faith, but we decided to implement an internal program: we wanted to create time and an official space for management and workers to meet, to enhance communication and relationship building. The idea was to set up a committee for local employees, as a new organ within our company structure. This Council would involve the company frontline employees, each one representing the different departments of the company. In our case, this meant different representatives for finance, purchasing, inventory, sales, human resources, and operations (Fig. 6.1).

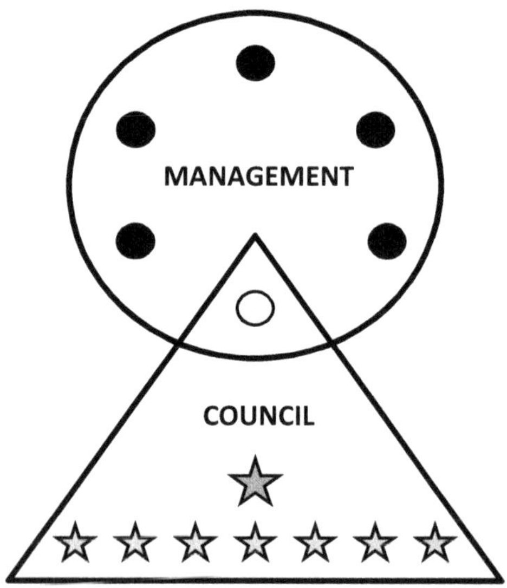

Fig. 6.1 A new Council within the organisational structure

The Council would be led by one of the local employees and this person would be allowed the freedom to set the agenda. The leader was meant to prepare and organize a monthly meeting, ensuring an equal participation among all the members and encouraging the free flow of information. On top, one of the managers would invest time and energy into the Council and take part in the deliberations.

Most of the time, this would be myself, as a Country Director. In order to involve other company managers and foremen as well, the Council Chairman would invite the presence of these people into their meeting, whenever necessary or appropriate.

At the moment of forming the Council, the management team was contemplating different names and 'Soba Council' was one of them, utilizing all the cultural associations and high norms for responsible behaviour and integrity that surrounds this specific type of leadership. At the first meeting, the Council members were to decide on the name. They would also nominate a secretary for preparing the meeting report that should be validated and signed by all members. The meeting decisions should be done by equal vote of each of the members, giving the Council Chairman the power to take the last uneven decision, in case of a draw of votes. The manager(s) being present at the time would not have voting power.

While the Soba's in the Angolan community often would be selected for a lifetime, in this case the Council members were expected to have a mandate of one year, in order to open up future participation for all other employees. However, in case the Council would decide that there is no other option among the department employees, the actual member could be designated for a new enrolment.

Rationale and Expectations from Management

We were hoping that the Council members would be able to act as 'natural' alpha leaders inside the company that could play a paramount role in helping us prevent the payment of further ignorance tax. The Council should also improve the management cultural knowledge regarding the informal structure and, mostly, encourage the collaboration from bottom-up. As a Country Director, one of my ideas for the Council was to provide management with further cultural insights and form a source of information within the loop of observation-interpretation-decision-action.

Fig. 6.2 Feedback loop

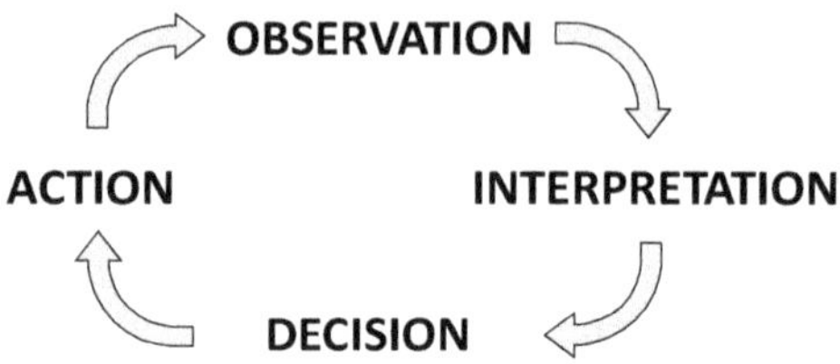

At the interpretation level, the Council would be able to give vital information to improve our decision-making preview (Fig. 6.2).

Moreover, Silva expected that the Council could play a paramount role in culture sensitive implementing of decisions and the definition of the right steps of action. After all, if decisions and information from the top are misunderstood, and in case they are based on stereotypes, assumed by superficial perceptions of culture sensitive topics, then chances are that this decision-making is inappropriate, that the priority of needs is poor, and that the organizational planning doesn't fit the reality on the ground.

The Council that we foresaw should not be confused with a Labour or Works Council, which are found in many Western companies. The reality is that this is exactly what we did not, and in fact did not want to, create.

Surely there are similarities between a Works Council and this new Council, but there are some significant and important differences as well. Once again (and we cannot stress it enough) cultural variance does not belong to the black and white domain, the differences are to be found in the details. At this stage, the case will be presented first, and these crucial nuances will be highlighted in the last chapter.

All in all, we were hoping that the Council would be able to:

- *Improve our employee's commitment (genuine, voluntary, and authentic) by making them part of the company community and granting power to managers from below.*
- *Show that (informal) hierarchies can also be 'natural' and that authority is fluid and should focus on value-added actions.*
- *Show all employees that capabilities are more important than credentials and titles.*
- *Improve the feedback flow from bottom-up and from top-down, by showing that managers can get personally involved (see figure below).*

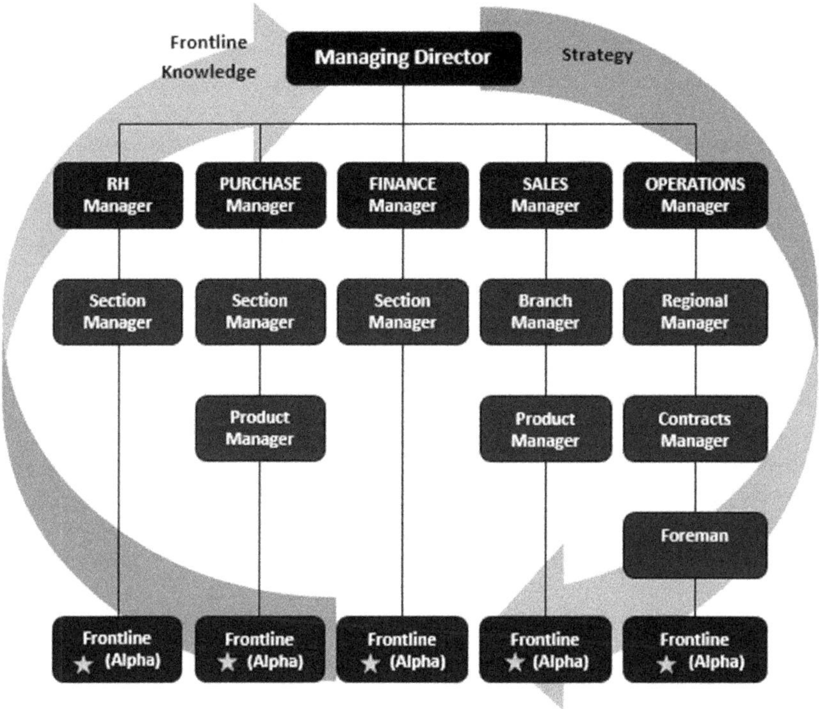

Fig. 6.3 Company knowledge and information flow—after intervention

- *Empower the company decision makers with fresh, raw and unfiltered information.*
- *Involve all employees for the corporate strategy definition and allow the available resources for improved decision-making grow exponentially.*
- *Finally, and most importantly, amplify our company human effort and achievement* (Fig. 6.3).

Selection of Members

One way for organizations to 'know' their employees is by using the information collected from performance evaluations by supervisors. This kind of information is quite limited though and can be compared to a book review of one or two pages. For every reader, it is obvious that the review does not reveal the precious insights hidden inside the book content. The same happens when expatriates perform appraisals and performance evaluations of a local workforce.

Do you know the informal structure of local employees within your company? What is the role of each local employee in this structure? Is there a local employee that is a 'natural' leader? In fact, relying on the superficial and incomplete information of an appraisal does not necessarily lead to good outputs.

Moreover, Hofstede has shown that appraisals and the related methodology of 'Management By Objectives' (MBO), with performance evaluations and expressed needs and wishes from an employee, may be less suitable for collectivist contexts. In such contexts, harmony and respect are prevalent, and without a proper defence or substantial dialogue (as is assumed in the USA where the methodology was developed), the reliability of the resulting written appraisals can be at risk.[1]

We realized that if the Council Chairman was not well selected, our company had high probability to miss the target of the organizational change.

Therefore, the team started by performing an HR analysis search for a frontline employee that could play the role of Chairman of the Council. The nomination was based on two sets of criteria:

1. They used the selection criteria that were found in the research for the Soba: high behaviour standards; genuine good character and intelligence; sense of justice and equal rights; leadership and communication qualities; and good decision-making skills.
2. They added some important criteria related to the company: full involvement with the company mission, values, and strategy; solid long-term career evolution inside the company; proven merit associated with high result achievements; and, finally, high influence skills towards peers, clients, and top management.

It was like searching for the Big Soba himself. We did go over the appraisals, but we also observed closely, and recalled and discussed many instances of the past, to tap into the informal structure that was already

[1] Hofstede (1980b).

present among our employees. In the end, it actually didn't prove to be very hard to find the right leader, because there's only a few people standing out in the crowd in this manner and my first talk with the person we had selected proved to be very promising. We discussed the concepts of representation and the Soba with him, which truly inspired him and visibly he started to take on a new leadership role.

The Chairman himself later remembers he was a bit reluctant at first: "Yes, I remember Mr. Vasco Silva speaking for the first time about the Council. My first reaction was that I questioned myself whether I should accept to participate in the meetings, because I thought it was about the creation of a union committee. I did not want that so at first, I hesitated. But after further clarification I was persuaded to accept the invitation, but in the beginning just to see what it would be like to be there."

After the acceptance of the Chairman, the management team asked him to nominate the other members, based on the same selection criteria presented before. In order to spread the influence through all frontline employees, the Chairman would nominate one member per department of the company. When asked afterwards, one of these members said: "I remember perfectly when the Country Director spoke about the Council for the first time. I was surprised, with a lot of anxiety and expectation. When asked to participate, it was a YES right away. Because I really wanted to know what the project had in store for us. I always thought it was a very promising idea at company level."

Generally, in Africa, with its variety of ethnicities within one country and borders drawn by the former colonizers, it is wise to know and consider the ethnicities of the employees and to understand individual and group behaviours and interactions fully. However, the selection of the Council members was based mainly on behaviour, influence, and results. In fact, Silva and the Council Chairman discussed and decided together not to push employees into an ethnic identity by selecting members based on geographical origin. This may not always be possible throughout the African continent though, as certain ethnic heritage could create strong bonds and in-groups (and out-groups) among the employees. Every manager in Africa is advised to pay attention to the way his workforce is spread over local groups or ethnicities and sometimes this may call for an ethnical selection condition. Upon asking by Vonk after one year of practice, different Council members explained that in the case of Luanda, however, people from a large variety of backgrounds had moved into the capital, largely due to the long civil war and regular rural-urban migration.

There was no majority of one ethnic group within the workforce, potentially threatening to dominate others. In the end, the Council turned out to be ethnically very diverse and they assured Vonk that ethnicity did not play any major role in the Council.

The First Meeting

After the selection of the Council members and the necessary communication executed throughout the company structure, it was time to perform the first Council meeting.

I particularly remember this moment very vividly. I left my office some five or ten minutes late and went to the meeting room. It was with a mixed sensation between the happiness of finally seeing the project being implemented and anxiety due to the increased complexity of the management and leadership skills that I would encounter in the future.

It remains a wonderful memory. As I entered the meeting room, I noticed that the Council members had placed the individual chairs in a circle. Indeed, the meeting could be held around a square or u-shaped table, but the Council members had put the tables aside and set the chairs to be organized in a figuratively round way. I believe the main interpretation was that there would be no hierarchical structure present in the meeting room, at least in principle. With this setting of chairs, there was no beginning, no end, top, bottom, or middle, and there was no leader at the head of the table. In the Council meetings, at its heart, everyone was considered equal, and there is simply a facilitator for support. From there on, participants could be comfortable and secure to express their opinions, share their experiences, and to be themselves. When our minds are open, and free of preconceptions, we learn and create. Everybody is there to ensure all participants have an opportunity to contribute and to keep the conversation flowing and focused.

This is not to say that there was no hierarchy in the room. The position of the Council Chairman and definitely the position as the Country Director were present in the deliberations that were to follow. This should be hardly surprising, seen in the light of our research findings of large power distance and acceptance of hierarchy, topped up with the continuous power of colonial hierarchies. As one of the members said: “It was very challenging to overcome shyness and apathy towards the hierarchical superior.” Albeit challenging, this turned out to become one of those spaces where everybody was allowed, even asked to speak freely and openly. This was also the place to give attention to the other side of the coin of high-power distance leadership: personal relationship building. The same member: "One of the good things were the open and frank debates on aspects that would improve the employer-employee relationship." The setting of the chairs provided an excellent space for this.

Naming the Council

In the first meeting, the name of the Council was discussed.

Based on the literature exploring the best practices of management and leadership, I remember that my original idea was to call it the Cult Committee. As a manager, I aimed at developing an inner company culture that can be described as a cult-like environment, where employee's behaviours and values can be differentiated easily from other companies. Team members would tend to work hard without prompting and would be less likely to be deterred by a challenge or a failure. They would want to do well not only for themselves but for their colleagues as well.

But the idea was not welcomed at all by the Council because the word 'Cult' in the Angolan culture context is associated with religion. The Council made it clear to me that in the Angolan culture, these are very distinct fields: religion is one and a corporation is essentially different (and predominantly secular).

This event was just my first Council 'slap in the face.' Imagine me, a European manager, communicating with my local workforce and saying that one of the main company tasks was to foster a cult-like culture. I am convinced that an average employee might have said 'yes' only as a sign of respect, but the execution would be zero because nobody would accept that a company culture could be a cult.

In fact, African society is full of cult-like groups and secret societies with magical powers and in retrospect it would have been haughty for the fresh Council members to claim such powers vis-à-vis their colleagues. The next proposal was to call this the Soba Council and use the titles of Soba for its members. After all, it was the institution of the Soba that had inspired both management team and some of the frontliners immensely, both in the formation of a council in the first place, as well as the criteria of its members in terms of ethics and integrity.

The members felt visibly honoured to be called Soba and by placing them at the core of their cultural heritage, it appealed to the norms and high standards of behaviour that is associated with this institution. At the same time, the frontliners also felt the title was a bit too loaded with meaning. They explained that the Soba was also associated with mystical powers. Moreover, the fact that a true Soba would be an older person, carrying the wisdom of the so-well respected elderly in African society, made some of them somewhat shy to carry this title at their young age.

The discussion showed once again that merging the contemporary traditional and the modern world cannot be done in an easy, straightforward motion. At that stage, consensus was reached on the official name 'Culture Council.' After all, the root idea was to culturally validate management decisions and develop culture sensitive actions to integrate the company as a whole. At the same time though, within the company the names Soba Council and Culture Council continued to be used alternately, as is done in this book. The Council members may have found it difficult to claim the name for themselves, yet they were honoured when others would apply the title to them. Also, during the Council meetings, the word Soba was often used, for instance in the quest for a reaction a true Soba would give to a certain situation. In this sense, the Soba remained an inspiration and a strong mirroring image to the Council members.

Mission and Values

During the second meeting, it was decided to formulate a Mission and Values statement for the Council. This resulted into an extensive and inclusive discussion of their general standards. The widely formulated statement was set to endure across management styles and procedures in the future. It was also during these deliberations that the image of the Soba spoke to the members and the gluing together of this new 'corporate community' became apparent (Table 6.1).

Activities

The centre piece of the Council was to be the monthly meeting, held on the last Tuesday of the month. These meetings would give members an opportunity to interact and provide them with the information and motivation they needed to increase their participation in activities that served the company as a whole. Monthly meetings started to feature an interesting agenda, with company-related issues that enhanced member's company knowledge, brainstorm ideas for projects and activities, reinforce

Table 6.1 Mission and values of the Culture Council

Mission and Values of the Culture Council	
1.	Foster the discussion of the company strategy, mission, values, and critical tasks throughout the company structure
2.	Ensure that every company employee has a voice and encourage the free communication within the company structure
3.	Support governance and counsel the company board, in order to improve the quality of the decisions, the impact, and the output
4.	Communicate a corporate message that states that the company belongs to all employees with the group motto: "Together for the company!"
5.	Prevent problems and surprises, by acting directly among all colleagues and providing all the needed information to decision makers
6.	Each member, in each department, strongly acts as a mentor for newcomers, in order to help their integration in the company and to anticipate results
7.	Members must act with candour, loyalty, and care towards the company, being recognized by all peers for their high behavioural standards
8.	Foster a human workplace, apart from high performance, people are incentivized to innovate and contribute, help each other, and have fun—Company Community
9.	All Culture Council members are supposed to be impartial, foster equal rights, fair justice, strong ethics, good judgement, and merit by example among all peers

the value of cultural insight and increase awareness of internal and external issues. A typical meeting started by the discussion of council activities, activities budgets and costs, governance and employees' issues and, finally, general information. To involve middle managers as well, the Chairman of the Council regularly asked them to be present in meetings.

One of the yearly Council tasks was to perform a discussion about the cultural sensitivity and execution of the company's vision, mission, values and behaviours.

The rationale of this task is that a brilliant strategy, an excellent service, or a breakthrough product can put a company on the competitive map, but the company only retains this competitive advantage with a solid execution strategy. Execution is the result of thousands of decisions made every day by employees, acting according to the information they have and their own self-interest. Therefore, the main objective of asking the Council to review the vision, mission, values, and behaviours was to gain cross-cultural insights and adapt the company's strategy to the local culture.

Another activity of the Culture Council was the organization of the company annual party. The members adjusted many aspects of this party in comparison with the way it was done before the existence of the Council and, as a climax event, they decided to offer (non-monetary) awards to some company employees.

Finally, the Culture Council chose to give more meaning to one of the company's values, being a socially responsible enterprise. They organized a social philanthropy activity, helping a needed community in Angola. In the next chapter, all these activities will be further elaborated, highlighting some of the most important and amazing results of the initiation of the Soba Council for the company.

Reference

Hofstede, G. (1980b). Motivation, leadership, and organization: Do American theories apply abroad? *Organizational Dynamics, 9*, 42–63.

CHAPTER 7

Reaping the Harvest: The Results of the Transformation

Abstract In this chapter, named 'Reaping the harvest,' the extensive results of a transformative organizational change process are reported. The one-and-half year of implementation of the Culture/Soba Council within a Portuguese subsidiary in Angola had created company trust and a community at company level. Decision making improved considerably, taking information from the bottom up and vice versa. Workers had found a space to express their needs; time was spent together, and relationships were built. Engagement and motivation went up visibly, and absenteeism and personnel turnover plummeted. Management observed innovative minds expressing themselves and emerging leadership skills they had not seen before. The yearly Company party improved enormously and the handing out of several awards gave the frontliners a chance to express their appreciation for certain colleagues as well as the possible lack of it for management. The evaluation of the Culture Council was very positive, except for a small minority who felt that the Council had a tendency for snitching.

Keywords Company trust · Community building · Absenteeism · Personnel turnover · Indigenous leadership · Company awards · Jesters

A. Vonk and V. F. Silva, *Cultural Confluence in Organizational Change*, Palgrave Studies in African Leadership,
https://doi.org/10.1007/978-3-031-45403-5_7

During that first one-and-a-half year of implementation of the program and the execution of activities of the Culture Council in the company, Silva and his workers experienced many interesting results, which will be shared in this chapter. The first paragraph will explain some of the structural results. Interesting anecdotes and occurrences about the information flow and about serving mutual interests will be outlined in the second paragraph. Thirdly, the organization of the events, with all their advantages for the company, will be described. After one year an evaluation was executed, and the outcomes and reflections of both Silva and the Council leader will be found in the fourth paragraph. The chapter ends with a few suggestions from Silva to improve the design and its execution.

Structural Achievements

Relationships

One of the main, possibly the most important, structural achievements was the improved relationships between the Country Director and the frontline employees. Time was spent together, conversation went back and forth, questions were asked, answers discussed, interest shown. This led to improved trust and actually did tie the company as a whole together. Information flow, motivation, and engagement all went up, which will become apparent in the course of this chapter.

As the Chairman of the Council explains: "For me, being part of the Culture Council was a very good experience. It was good for me, as a Chairman, to contribute to a unifying spirit among the employees. The Council meetings and the implementation of the issues discussed put all employees on the same level, as fundamental pieces for the growth of the company. Listening and giving voice to the wishes and concerns of all, helped me in part to better know and interact with everyone, from the Director to the basic worker of the company."

Individual Leadership and Capabilities

Silva: Throughout the year, we discovered skills and capabilities in some of our employees that we never noticed before. We saw new leadership skills emerge among several of the Council members. Probably because of the cultural difference in relation to power, some of the workers had seemed introvert to us, or we were of the impression that they were not involved with their work. Within the Council they seemed to become alive, take positions, and they proved to be very able to convince others and lead the way. We observed innovative minds, finding new solutions that we would have never thought of ourselves.

Silva also came to know the organization's 'jesters.' As Vonk has explained elsewhere: especially within a collectivist, large power distance and indulgent culture (like Angola), a 'jester' is often a blessing for a team or an organization. Since there is high respect for leadership and a strong need to maintain harmony, it is not always easy for an inconvenient truth to come to the table. With the indulgent aspect of their culture though, humour is highly valued, which means that if somebody is capable of packaging the truth inside a funny joke, it becomes more acceptable. A jester, therefore, does not only do wonders for a good atmosphere, he or she may tell you something that others will not.[1]

Dandala, in his article about embracing African cosmology in the process of economic growth, explains a similar role found in South Africa: "There are checkpoints within the system through which the chiefs' shortcomings or mistakes may be drawn to his attention. This takes place through the institution of the praise-singer (...). He is the official interpreter of the context of the governance of the chief, similar to a journalist today (Qwelane, 1995)."[2]

Silva: All in all, the Council members took their new role with skill, initiative, and impetus.

A Shared Company Mission

Another fundamental change that Silva observed was that the Culture Council meetings became accustomed to discussing the Company mission, values, and strategy. After the Council had established its own mission and values in one of their first meetings, they also studied the vision, mission, and values statements for the whole Company, that had been proposed by management. They did not necessarily change them, but discussed their interpretation, putting these statements into their own words and emphasizing the ones that stood out for them.

[1] Vonk (2016, p. 18; 2017, p. 30), and Meertens (2017, p. 193).

[2] Dandala (2009, p. 267).

Apart from making these statements part of their vocabulary, we noticed that they automatically started to discuss them with their co-workers in their respective departments. Actually, we observed that <u>*all*</u> *the frontline employees started to discuss the vision, mission, and values of the company and since then became more involved.*

Moreover, the Culture Council implementation resulted in an improved onboarding of new employees, leading to lower integration times and improved company outputs.

Our Culture Council members, in each department, acted extremely well as newcomer's mentors, clarifying in-person issues such as corporate culture, extra-time measurement procedures, wage payment days, the need for documents to justify faults, company events, company norms, values, mission, and vision. Before the implementation of the Culture Council, we had several employees leaving their construction site, in order to come to office to ask explanations about their salary payment receipts. The Council members prevented this by explaining in detail how the wages were calculated, including the extra-time hours. With the spread of information and delegation of mentorship roles, the company prevented the waste of time and resources.

In fact, the overall absenteeism came down from 2.4% in the year prior to the implementation of the Soba Committee to 0.7% in the year following its establishment (Fig. 7.1).

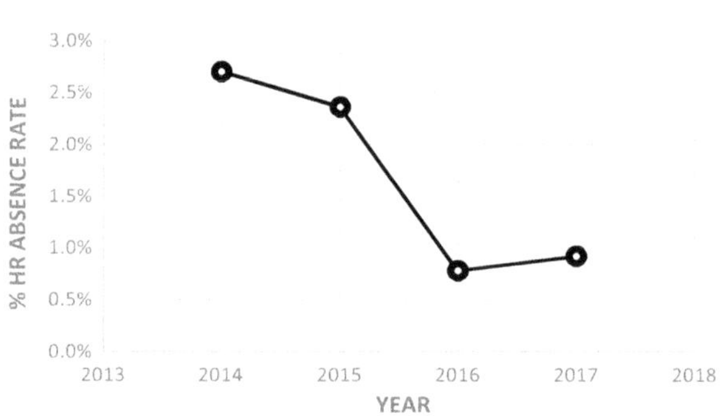

Fig. 7.1 Decrease of absenteeism

Practical Needs

Over the year, practical valuable bottom-up knowledge surfaced during the Council meetings, which improved the company's governance and its decision-making. Examples are for instance the local per diem or daily allowances for work executed outside Luanda; protective clothing, such as work boots and specs; the continued discussion about extra-time hours and input about the transportation regulations to the construction sites. These discussions made it much clearer to management what the frontliners needed to execute their jobs effectively and efficiently.

And it was the involvement of the Council members with the company and with its strategy, which made these requests reasonable and responsible.

Cultural Insights

On top, the Cultural Council continued to explain to me and the *other managers the local, cultural practices of which we had no knowledge. To mention an example, we discussed the failed implementation of a financial assistance program for the employees from our HR department. Within that program the company had offered to advance 50% of the monthly salary to any employee, if requested. The reason for this program was the economic crisis that had followed the reduction of the price of crude oil in 2014 to its lowest level in more than a decade. It had pushed Angola's currency to record lows and had plunged the economy of Africa's second largest crude oil producer into severe difficulty. Apart from leading to a great reduction in economic activity, we had noticed also severe difficulties in our workforce to deal with this economic downturn. In fact, Angola suffers endemic poverty, with more than a third of the population of around 24 million living below the poverty line, according to the United Nations.*[3] *As a company, we saw the 50% advance of the monthly salary as a social corporate responsibility and part of our commitments to contribute to the quality of life of our workforce and their families. We had asked some workers whether they would like it and we had interpreted the answers as confirmative. However, in retrospect we may conclude that these answers had probably been formulated in indirect and respectful manner and could now be categorized as ceremonial adoption, mentioned earlier. Because after two to three months implementation of the financial assistance program, the effect was almost negligible,*

[3] United Nations Development Programme (UNDP).

receiving only one or two requests from a workforce of 80 people. We were surprised and just could not understand why most employees didn't ask for this 50% advance right after the launch.

I decided to ask the Culture Council about this program and try to disclose the unknown cultural reasons for the poor results in execution. The answer from the members was consensual and very accurate. They explained to me that the reason for the lack of success was a traditional saving system that locals have, named Kichinguila. To my amazement I came to understand that it is very common that groups of three or four employees collect their monthly wage and deliver the total amount to one member of this group. The leverage procedure provides this person with the liquidity to invest in some personal business, asset, or expense: refurbishment of house, motorcycle, medical, business, or land. Naturally, it's a rotating system, whereby each month another one of the group receives the total amount. When the company tried to advance 50% of the salary, it would break this chain and the employees would not be able to honour their agreement to pay the full salary at the end of the month to the Kichinguila group. Little did we know that such saving schemes can be found throughout Africa below the Sahara: we had learned another lesson here.

This occasion showed even more the necessity of presenting Board decisions to the Culture Council in advance for culture-context validation, in order to have proper prediction of execution outputs.

Information Flow and Serving Mutual Interests

In the beginning of this chapter I mentioned that among the main structural achievements were the improved relationships between management and me as a Country Director, on the one hand, and the frontline employees and foremen, on the other. In turn, this led to increased trust and to an improved information flow.

The Chairman of the Council explains: "The creation of the companies' Cultural Council has been very useful for both the people and the company. People work better together when they know each other and when the work goes well, both the company and the employees win."

Knowing each other improved the information flow and the benefits worked both ways. Sometimes the Country Director and the management team were able to meet the wishes of the employees; at other times they could express their concerns and request collaboration from the Council members.

One such incident is the painful leave of one of our managers. There was a black cloud in my mind, fearing that he could invite our best employees to leave and go along with him, offering a better salary and incentives conditions. We were convinced by now that our employees were committed to the company mission and values and we were a 100% sure that our salary policy was sound, compared to our competitors. However, we knew that we were in a culturally strange, and therefore unpredictable environment so at least the direct subordinates of the leaving manager might want to follow him, and our company could lose its most precious asset: the local and trained employees. The Culture Council played an important role since the issue was discussed at length during the meetings and the members agreed to take their responsibility and be very attentive to their colleagues to prevent them from leaving the company. In the end, we came to know that the manager in question did present several proposals to some of our employees with better conditions, yet all the employees remained loyal to our company.

In fact, generally the turnover of the workforce plummeted, from 2.86% the year before the Soba Committee was put into place, to 1.12% of the year that followed and even 0.58% one year later (Fig. 7.2).

Another workforce event disclosed within the Culture Council was related to the dismissal of three employees due to excess of work absence and, consequently, lack of performance. Just by the end of one of the Cultural Council meetings, we were already preparing to leave the room, the Chairman asked for permission to speak about an issue that was disturbing the company. He stated that it was known that three employees were dismissed from the company last month. However, one of these individuals had been facing

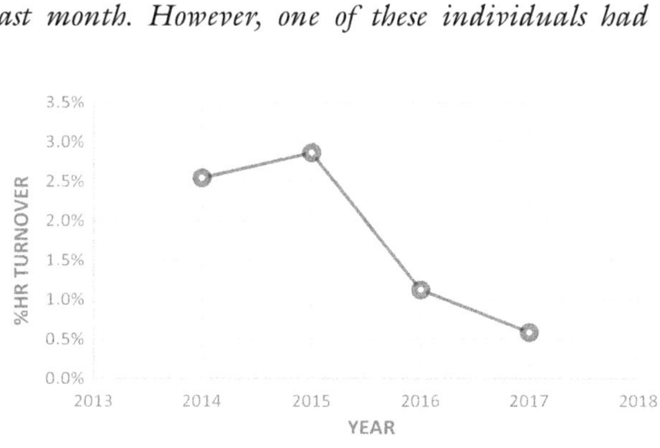

Fig. 7.2 Decrease of personnel turnover

severe financial problems and the Council believed this had been the reason for the lack of performance. Also, the Chairman mentioned that there had been serious family issues and the employee had been going through a very tough time. After the meeting, I tried to get some middle management feedback about this employee and spoke with the foreman and operations manager. After ensuring that a second chance for this employee would be financially possible and would not jeopardize the company operations, values, and rules, the management team decided to reincorporate the employee. This decision was presented during a Culture Council meeting and the deal was that the members would mentor the behaviour of the employee and ensure that the company would not have any further problems with him.

When asked what was the best thing that the Culture Council had done, one of the members answered: "Reaching out to the General Management and respectfully asking them to reconsider the decision to dismiss an employee which many felt was a little unfair. And that's what happened. It was a very remarkable and unforgettable moment."

Moreover, still in the context of the candour, loyalty, and care of the Council members towards the company, I'd like to share a second version of the shocking event that is presented in the introduction of this book. After a day of hard work, I received a late call from a member of the Culture Council. The person stated that a group of employees was planning to stop doing the extra-time hours. There seemed to be an issue with one of our most important projects since the establishment of our Company. The work value of this project was nearly four times the one we executed during the earlier wild strike, and it was set to be finishing in the few weeks following this phone call conversation. We already felt the pressure of this large project and the last thing we could use was another strike! It turned out there was a technical issue with one of our company vans. The van was scheduled to be at the construction site by the end of each day to collect all employees and take them home, one by one. In Angola, there's almost no public transport services and our employees live inside unsafe, very crowded and remote places, without the existence of conventional infrastructures (roads, walkways or light). Of course, immediately after the call, I spoke with both the operations manager and the logistics manager and the last was able to arrange an extra van to ensure the timely transportation of all employees. The exemplar behaviour of the Council member was then presented as a role model to follow and replicate in the Council meeting, and similar attention was expected from other members in future critical events for the company.

Finally, one more incident is worth mentioning. By the end of another Culture Council meeting, the Chairman asked if there was any additional issue that the members wanted to communicate. Again, we were all just preparing to return to work, when one of the members asked for permission to speak. After granted permission, he stated that several co-workers had come to him, complaining about the behaviour of one of the foremen. He explained that this foreman exhibited bad behaviour with several local employees, following a very strict and authoritarian leadership style and sometimes being on the threshold of disrespect and insult. In fact, nobody wanted to work with him, I was told. After finishing the meeting, I went to my management team to get more information. The reality was that the foreman was already known for this behaviour and did not seem to be interested in adapting or changing his behaviour. We tried to influence his transformation, but without success and in the end, as a result, we could not renew our labour contract with the person. As such, we tried to ensure that our workplace remained a place where all our employees were able to feel valued and treated with the proper respect.

The Annual Company Ceremony

One of the annual tasks of the Soba Committee was to organize the company annual festivity according to the best local cultural practices. Previously, a small event had been organized, but the impact on employees had been disappointing. Angola has a good tradition of organizing parties, but the organization of the annual event based on European standards had led to poor execution and results.

I remember having an exhausting evening, doing everything by myself and I remember the eager employees waiting to take their children's presents and walk home.

The event had been called the Christmas Party of the company, but the Council made it clear that this name was not welcomed by some employees, since they were not Catholic and hence, they felt excluded (Jehovah's Witnesses, Evangelic, etc.). The change of name into "the Annual Company Ceremony" enabled a much more inclusive event. Even the selection of the hour for the event proved to be inappropriate according to the Soba Council, because late hours meant increased difficulties for the employees to get back home.

In earlier years we had started to offer presents to the children of the employees. Prior two weeks to the event, we had asked for the names of the sons and daughters of the employees and arranged the purchase of one present for each, taking their ages into account. The reason for this is that I had had the opportunity to visit some employee's homes and always noticed the absence of toys. Thus, the Company Board had full consensus in offering presents to the employee's children. However, to our surprise, the Soba Council informed us that during those past events some employees had presented the names of nephews, cousins, even neighbours! According to the members, these people had incorrectly collected presents from the company. Therefore, the Council decided to start asking for the child registration documents to prove their parenthood over the children. This decision caused an incredible discomfort among employees because in Angola not all children are being registered after birth. To my surprise, the Soba Council kept committed to their decision and employees had to arrange travels to different provinces to register their sons and daughters.

In the renewed 'Annual Company Ceremony,' there were new elements as well, such as music, dance, and a theatre act. The Chairman, or our 'Big Soba,' as he was regularly called, acted as a fantastic event host. When he was asked a few years later about the Culture Council, he referred to the dignity and equality these Ceremonies displayed: "In my point of view the best thing the Culture Council did was giving no room for social classes or levels among employees, spouses and children. Even though I am no longer at the company, my children still ask me to visit the company." He also referred to these occasions as one of the drivers for the acceptance of the Culture Council among other employees.

The climax of the Annual Company Ceremony was the presentation of the non-monetary awards to the company employees, comprising the following categories:

- Tutor—Foreman or manager recognized for being the best trainer, coach or teacher.
- Professionalism—Employee recognized by all to be 200% involved with the Company's vision, mission, values, and behaviours.
- Promise—High potential employee with less than 2 years in the Company.
- Gratitude—Employee with exemplar behaviour and a respectful number of years within the Company.
- Personality—Employee with good contribution to the Company, highly respected by colleagues and clients.

- Evolution—Employee with the most remarkable career evolution inside the Company.

After the first year, the prize Gratitude was replaced by the prize named 'Kamba' (meaning 'friend' in Angola dialect), to appraise the employee that had always been available to collaborate with everybody and had been helping to solve complex, technical problems.

For me as a Country Director, one impressive event of the year was the all-day meeting of the Soba Council, exclusively dedicated to the preparations of these awards. This meeting provided me access to very valuable information regarding employee's performance, in a 360-degree appraisal, with classifications and discussion regarding several aspects: evolution, tutorship, personality, professionalism, gratitude ('kamba'), and future career promise. For each price category and within their meeting, the Council nominated three candidates and a poll was then obtained. Among a wealth of other information, I understood which expatriate was most respected by the local employees, which junior talented employees were promising in terms of evolution inside the company structure, which employee represented most the values and mission of the company and which employee was believed to have been promoted for the hard work and intelligence, rather than passing duties on to other colleagues.

After these meetings, I stepped out of the room with a completely new lens looking at our workforce, including both expatriates and locals. Whenever appropriate, I passed some of the positive information on, both to HR and to the operations department, increasing the company's attention towards these employees in order to foster even more growth and talent management.

Despite obtaining these insights, I remember feeling a bit at odds as well. I wasn't always 100 % at ease with this complete free flow of information about colleagues. Indeed, as we will see in the evaluation, there were a few voices referring to the Council members as 'snitchers.' Luckily, such statement represented a small minority. The Council members did not seem bothered by my presence and after all, they were primarily talking about all the ups and positive sides of their colleagues during these conversations. Still, the 'Big Soba' addressed this accusation of snitching publicly, at the first Annual Company Ceremony. He urged his colleagues not to look upon them as snitchers, but rather look at them as their representatives: all employees could use them as their channel towards management and the Council existed to support the company for the good of all.

Concerning the award ceremony itself, it must be said that Angolan culture is not known for singling out one individual from the community and putting him/her in the limelight and, being both feminine and collectivist, the people generally care more about cooperation and consensus among all. Still, the existence of the annual recognition awards had quite some impact on the general employee's behaviour.

It was easy to notice the efforts of all employees, including expats, towards the next year awards nomination. The youngsters tried to work even harder and to contribute with extra effort towards the company interests and strategy.

The most important gain of the awards was the fact that power was handed down to the frontlines, building a bottom-up bridge for recognition and appraisal. Some foremen and managers (mostly expats) were also granted with prizes, enabling the frontlines appraisal for the ones who adapted best to the local culture and, according to them, performed best in the interest of the company.

There was always a healthy tension during the Annual Company Ceremony, at that moment just before the Chairman presented the winners of the prizes. Especially for the ones for tutor, professionalism, and personality: the Portuguese managers were looking at each other, trying to get the recognition from the local employees. As a result, we noticed great evolution in expatriates' behaviour and performance, trying to act as mentors and technical trainers for the young locals and frontline workers, with respect for the local culture, and performing with the whole company in mind, instead of only top management.

The Humanitarian Activity

As a complement to the Annual Company Event, the company's anniversary was also celebrated and the Soba Council had asked to organize a social humanitarian activity to assist a community in need in Angola. In one of the meetings, the Council was challenged to identify a community that could be assisted by our company. Another option that came to mind was to develop some action inside the company, to support some employees that were facing problems, but the Council decided that the humanitarian event should be organized outside the company. Therefore, after the presentation of several options, a rural community of Kileba, Muxima was selected, which is located around 100 miles from Luanda. One Council member contacted the Priest of the Muxima Area, which is a well-known holy place in the countryside of Angola. The Priest stated that usually this community consumed untreated plain water from surface wells that caused health problems, such as diarrhoea, gastric issues, dehydration, fever, digestion and, in some cases, death, mainly for new-borns, babies, and children. Thus, the Council planned to deliver 100 units of water filters, which would enable the community to have safe drinking water. The plan for the event was performed in detail, accounting for the employees, vehicles, food, and drivers. From the beginning the Council decided that the delivery of the water filters should be done directly to the final users and not to use any intermediaries.

Travelling to the community place was a challenge for the team. The last 30 miles was on untarred road, while, with 20 employees, we were tucked into four-wheel-drive SUVs and a pickup. When we finally reached the village, the sensation was amazing for all of us. It was a beautiful rural place, the inhabitants were very friendly, and they warmly welcomed the company employees, who later confided in me that they had felt afraid at first.

After the greetings, we were all seated inside the school building for the water filters delivery event. The Council members started by introducing the company and the humanitarian objective of their coming. They presented the water filters and described how they should be used. Some of the employees used the community dialects in order to ease the communication. As a foreigner, I was just amazed by the moment and touched by the privilege to participate in the event.

Apart from the social impact, this event acted also for team motivation, team building, and learning about social responsibility. When several months later, the Council members were asked for their best experience in the Council, many of them mentioned this activity: "I never thought we would be able to do such a thing in a rural place like that."

Succession

A critical issue that was discussed at length inside the Soba Council was the member's succession. As mentioned before, the Council members were expected to have a mandate of one year in order to keep the future participation open for all other employees. However, after one year of membership, the Country Director decided to bring the issue up for discussion again and get opinions regarding the coming years. After all, an actual Soba is selected for a lifetime and generally the experience gained by leaders is highly valued and leadership lasts long. In fact, many of the members indeed would have liked to continue, and this issue created a debate that lasted for some time. Some of the members wanted the current Council to stay into service, arguing that one year is very short for truthful development and that there would be a loss of gained experience. Possibly they also found it hard to lose the status they had gained as a Council member.

At first the Council decided to follow this line of argument and they decided that the current members would stay in their role for one more year. However, at the following meeting the majority had changed their mind and five out of seven members stated that the Council members had received a one-year mandate from the start and that it was important to keep consistent with the message presented to all employees when the Council was created. They did not think it would look good towards their colleagues if they came to know that the members had decided to stay in the Council for another year and block their participation. Consensus was reached to stick to the one-year mandate, except for one member, who would remain and become the new Chairman, to transmit the gained experience to others. Every other member nominated its substitute, and with only three months delay, the new membership was granted during the second Annual Company Ceremony.

The new members received their nomination with both honour and happiness all over their faces and they took up their new positions and tasks with the same vigour the first group had done.

The first Chairman: "In the beginning (of the Culture Council) there was a lot of unease on the part of colleagues, but after a few meetings with the collective of workers, including their spouses and children, there was a lot of interest from colleagues to participate in the council as well."

Evaluation of Internal Stakeholders

After one year a qualitative evaluation was executed, and the perspectives and observations of the employees about the impact of the Soba Council were mapped out. Both Vonk and Silva interviewed several employees (both members and non-members of the Council; both frontliners, foremen, and managers) and compiled their views. This was done separately for the frontline workers, on the one hand, and foremen and middle management, on the other. The Country Director added his points of evaluation to the list. All groups commented on both the positives and the negatives of the intervention.

The most important advantage for the frontline workers, which was repeated by many of them, was that the Soba Council ensured a voice for every company employee and that it encouraged contacts and information to flow within the company. They mentioned that it improved their access to and influence on the decisions of management. Labour conditions like their gear and transport improved. The frontliners appreciated the fact that the workplace seemed to have become more 'human' with genuine personal interests into one another; they liked the idea of being a family and they had the feeling that they belonged more than they did previously. Along those lines, some of them also mentioned that they had learned through the Council far better what the company was about and how the good work of one impacted the good of all. They also mentioned that they were happy that there was a place where they could address behavioural problems (lack of respect, accounting for extra work hours, and lack of transport were mentioned). Also, the considerable improvement of the Company Annual Ceremony had not gone unnoticed, especially with the performance of an active culture organization. Finally, the frontline workers mentioned the execution of a social responsibility activity to help needed communities, as a positive.

On the negative side, some frontline workers commented that there had been some misunderstandings and issues with Foremen and Middle managers regarding time allocation for the Council. After all, the Council members had to leave the construction sites for the meetings, and there were a few occasions where the managers had forgotten about it.

Another negative was that a few employees still stated that Soba Council members were company snitchers, as we observed earlier, and one frontliner once said it publicly, during one of the Company Annual Ceremonies. This opinion seemed to be held by a clear minority though. A Council member: "In my opinion, 90% of colleagues gave the project their full support, and it was very well accepted." Albeit coming from a minority, this remained one of the criticisms of the Council.

A third negative, which might be related, is expressed in the following quote of the first Chairman: "The sad thing about the Council was partly the misunderstanding by some colleagues who saw the representative members as the favoured ones of the company, just for the simple fact that we could stop to meet on certain occasions and have a meal together after such meetings." This is also an interesting pushback and sounds like a form of jealousy, which was discussed in Chapter 4, possibly related to the collectivist pressure to share and not to gain or attract more goods or food than others.[4] That is a speculation, of course. It does throw some light on the circumstances the Council members had to deal with and the pressure they encountered in their new role from their peers. From a positive viewpoint, one might also interpret these 'negatives' as actual proof of innovation taking place: it's hard to imagine deep change without some criticasters and disapproval.

In retrospect, such criticism may have also influenced the acceptance of the title of Soba. When Vonk interviewed the Council members after one year and asked whether they felt like a Soba, the majority reacted quite shy to fully accept the title. Some were in doubt, a few others shook their head with a smile, indicating: "no not really," and two members answered the question with an outright "yes." A few years later, the Chairman commented on one of the downsides of the name Soba: "It gave other people the opportunity to think of us as the favoured ones in the company."

All in all, though, the majority of the frontliners, members as well as non-members, were positive about the Culture Council. According to one member: "The creation of the Council was useful for the employees and for the company. I saw that the Council destroyed some hills that made employees feel distant from the company and created bridges that made even the smallest employees feel more valued."

For the Foremen and Middle Management (both expatriates and local), the evaluation was mostly positive as well. The most important benefit for them was the prevention of problems and surprises, by an improved flow of information bottom-up and top-down and by the provision of valuable information for efficient decision making. They appreciated the improved culture sensitive organization of the company, shown both by the annual ceremony and the social responsibility event by the Council members, to help remote needed communities. The appraisal of expatriate employees by local employees, with the granting of prizes, within the category's tutorship, personality, and professionalism, was mentioned frequently. Last but not least, they had noticed higher levels of motivation of local workforce, ensuring the company's ability to attract, retain and leverage local human resources.

A disadvantage, according to Foremen and Middle Management, was the higher level of management complexity: information and requests

[4] Noorderhaven and Tidjani (2001).

now came from all sides, both from HQ and from local workers; both from the top and from the bottom. Secondly, they mentioned a few problems concerning the timely communication of the Soba Council meetings, leading to complications for the planning and allocation of human resources.

For me as the Country Director, the only disadvantage was the higher level of management and leadership complexity due to multiple cultural and strategic realities on both global and local levels. Apart from this disadvantage, which proved to be an interesting challenge, the benefits were numerous and can be listed as follows:

- *Prevention of problems and surprises, by an improved flow of information bottom-up and top-down and providing valuable information for efficient decision making.*
- *More ownership of the company strategy, mission, critical tasks, and values throughout the company structure, building a higher calibre organization.*
- *Drop of absenteeism at the workplace.*
- *The Council members strongly acted as a mentor for the newcomers, which supported their integration into the company, leading to result achievements.*
- *Help and counsel the company board and governance, to improve the decisions quality, impact, and outputs.*
- *Improved local cultural active organization of the company annual conference and social responsibility event by the Soba Council members.*
- *Access to very valuable information regarding employee's performance 360º appraisal by several aspects: evolution, tutorship, personality, professionalism, gratitude, and future career promise.*
- *Creation of a human-like workplace with more respect for local employees, improving the operations control of foreman's and middle management.*
- *Higher levels of motivation of local workforce, ensuring the company ability to attract, retain, and leverage local human resources.*

Here I would like to add two pieces of reflection for the future. The first is that although the Council meeting with the selection of award winners was very valuable to me, each time leaving the room looking at the workforce with new eyes and improved ability to recognize new talent, I would consider leaving the Council to do these deliberations without management presence. After all, it remains sensitive information being shared, and we would still see the overall outcome. This may alleviate the (marginal, yet present) accusation of members being snitchers.

Secondly, the Council formed a complicating factor for middle management. For once they had to manage more complex time schedules, due to the time Council members spent in their meetings, as was put forward in the evaluation. More importantly, although both Council members and I involved middle management on many occasions, it remains true that we were 'jumping the pyramid,' and they could have felt bypassed at times. Overall, things went well, and they didn't mention it in the evaluation, but it may be advisable to allocate them a more structural role. For instance, by alternately putting their field of responsibility on the agenda, so they will have an allocated time to discuss their area of operation.

In total, the evaluation is very positive from all stakeholders, and it can be concluded that the company has been able to implement a culture-specific intervention that has integrated the workforce much further into the company as a whole. By establishing personal relationships, merging with indigenous role models, and handing down a certain amount of power to the front lines, they had truly become a more joyful and culturally centred workplace, which has supported belonging, growth and performance.

References

Dandala, M. (2009). Cows never die: Embracing African cosmology in the process of economic growth. In M. F. Murove (Ed.), *African ethics: An anthology of comparative and applied ethics* (pp. 259–277). KwaZulu-Natal Press.

Meertens, J.V. (2017). *Do we have a deal? - Succesvol onderhandelen in andere culturen*. Zaltbommel, the Netherlands: Haystack.

Noorderhaven, N.G. & Tidjani, B. (2001). Culture, Governance, and Economic Performance: An Explorative Study with a special focus on Africa. *International Journal of Cross Cultural Management 1*(1): 31-52.

Vonk, A. P. (2016). OD approaches in other cultures. *OD Practitioner, 48*(3), 13–21.

Vonk, A. P. (2017). Interactieve benaderingen langs de culturele meetlat. *M&O, 71*(1), 21–35.

PART IV

Conclusion

With a proper shift towards a geocentric company profile, our company has been able to transform the uncertainty and cultural risks into a huge opportunity and link this part of our risk managementstrategy to our corporate mission and codes of conduct. In a multicultural setting, this asks for the incorporation of elements of both national cultures, to form a truly hybrid organizational culture. With thus negotiated shared vision, values, and beliefs at its heart, culture serves as a compass setting, steering people in a common direction and providing rules that govern human interactions.

The establishment of the Culture Council and the organizational change that took place have been described in depth in the previous Part. This last Part contains only one chapter. It will analyse this case some steps further, taking the discussion forward into the future. The first paragraph will sift out a few general lessons learned about the confluence of the 'contemporary traditional' and 'modernity' taking place on the African continent. Subsequently, a more detailed question will be posed: What have been the exact adaptations from the Portuguese side and from the Angolan side? What has actually changed vis-à-vis their original forms, to bridge the gap, for the two worlds to come together and click? In other words, what are the performative, flexible elements in this specific story, both from the African as well as the European perspective? This question will be answered at an organizational and at a leadership level. At organizational level, the differences between the Culture Council and a Works or Union Council will be analysed. This will be followed by paragraphs on leadership, whereby the adaptation for both African and European leadership will be discussed: the case of the Soba Council and lessons concerning African leadership, and the consequences for western leadership on the African continent. Finally, this chapter returns to geocentric management, which was discussed in Chapter 2. The consequences of the case study for the HR department of any MNC will be commented upon, and at the end of his journey, Silva looks back with a few meaningful concluding remarks.

CHAPTER 8

Spaces of Cultural Confluence: Performative Elements of Leadership

Abstract Part IV is the conclusion and embodies one chapter, with a wrap-up and taking some lessons into the future. One of the conclusions is that diversity, many-faceted identities and structures, duplication of institutions, already existing as well as emerging complementarity between the modern and the traditional aspects: they all seem to be part of African reality today. Furthermore, the Culture/Soba Council is significantly different from a Works Council because of the nature of the dialogue, being harmonious and avoiding discussion or confrontation; because of the cultural exchange; the relationship building; and the striving for the common good along community guidelines. While rather essentialist values concerning collectivism and power distance remained in tact, the Angolan performative aspects were observed in the flexibility in hierarchical thinking: accepting this company space as a place to speak up; enacting a leadership (even Soba) role while being young, possibly female; and handing it on to others after one year. The main performative aspect for Portuguese leadership was embracing more complexity and building genuine relationships at all levels. The chapter ends with some consequences for HR departments and with some final remarks from Silva.

A. Vonk and V. F. Silva, *Cultural Confluence in Organizational Change*, Palgrave Studies in African Leadership,
https://doi.org/10.1007/978-3-031-45403-5_8

Keywords African leadership · Geocentric leadership · Performative culture · Works Council · Union Council · Company Community building · Multinational HR

Contemporary Tradition, Modernity, or Confluence?

The Culture Council forms an interesting case of the combination of (contemporary) traditional concepts of Angola with the practices of a foreign private company, striving for production and providing a livelihood for its employees in the modern economy. As such it can be considered an example of a much larger strive for cultural integration on the African continent. On this huge continent with its multifocal cultural environment, we have seen that it remains an ongoing discussion which way to turn; either to first look back, studying deeply rooted patterns of community, leadership, ethics, and governance to build upon; or to enter and embrace the modern world fully and strive for modernity in all aspects of the African life.

As mentioned, some believe that it will be 'traditional logic' of Africa that will ultimately dominate the cultural landscape of sub-Saharan Africa. Two arguments which would underpin such a statement were mentioned in the course of the past chapters. For instance, many scholars consider culture a deep, unconscious, and all-consuming force. Hofstede and other authors in his footsteps found that at least the relative basic assumptions and deeper values (i.e. the core of the onion) of different peoples in the world show quite a remarkable stability, at times even over centuries.[1] For once, culture is to a large extent unconsciously passed from one generation to the next, but also when pointed out, most peoples on the African continent are content and proud of cultural features like collectivism for instance.

Secondly, it was found that many African countries show a culture that is characterised by a relative short-term orientation, as compared to other countries. This cultural dimension correlated nearly perfectly with the

[1] Hofstede et al., (2010, p. 34), Beugelsdijk and Welzel (2018), Hofstede (2019), and Kirkman et al. (2006).

dimension of 'Traditional wisdom' formulated by African scholars. They suggest a tendency to perceive the past and traditions as very attractive sources of inspiration for decisions to be taken in the present. It is imaginable that this generally shared score has been reinforced because of the cultural disarray during and after slavery and colonialization, leading to a profoundly felt necessity to restore the links with the past and/or to restore the links to their own humanity. At the same time, this cultural trait might also make it more challenging to merge the different systems in a pragmatic manner, as cultures with a low average score on LTO, in their strive for stability, tend to be more normative (essentialist), rather than flexible (performative).

At the same time, the opposite arguments were found as well. Modernity and cosmopolitanism seem to have entered deeply into the veins of Africa. The nation state, the church and the mosque, ministries, NGO's and large-scale companies, they are all part of the landscape today and we could enlarge the list with an enormity of other institutions and practices. It is 'modernity' which facilitates the relationships between Africa and the rest of the world. More importantly, we've cited several African scholars embracing modernity, yearning to look into the future. Certainly, most Africans do not want to be trapped in "old barbarism"[2] and prefer to leave at least certain aspects of their heritage behind and see modernity as an attractive promise.

Consequently, the very question to make a conclusive 'choice' between these different cultural complexes is quite presumptuous, not necessary, nor even possible. Moreover, it's also been found that although the notions of tradition and modernity are vividly alive in people's minds, they remain constructs with so much overlap and internal contradictions, that they hardly hold as distinct bodies of logic.[3] Therefore, diversity, many-faceted identities and structures, duplication of institutions, already existing as well as emerging complementarity and merging processes: they all seem to be part of African reality today.

[2] Eze (2010, p. 120).

[3] Geschiere et al. (2009).

The Soba Council vs. the Works or Union Council

The Soba Council in our example can be studied as such a confluence of cultural notions, making use of the indigenous name and making an appeal to its associated values and behaviour, yet taking place within a Portuguese company following Western forms of decision making and communication. Of course, it is a very humble example, sitting in its own little niche. But the question asked is: Can we consider the establishment of the Soba Council open ended; did it create space for true dialogue and did a new, shared narrative arise? In other words, can we speak of a performative conception of the Soba Council and of Portuguese, foreign management?

This question will be answered through a comparison between the Culture Council and a Works Council, common in many western companies and beyond, and also found in Multinational companies in Africa. In Chapter 6, the question was already posed whether the Culture Council is different from a Works Council. Surely there are similarities between these structures, yet they are certainly not identical. In this case, as in many cases, cultural differences can often be found in seemingly small, but crucial details.

Generally, the rationale of a Works Council is to allow the critical voices within the workforce to speak up, it is to institutionalize bargaining power of workers vis-à-vis their management. The Works Council, we may say, organizes the pushback, the opposition, the antithesis. As such it is based on rather confrontational cultural assumptions, with the necessity for employees to communicate in a somewhat direct manner to management, even to oppose management as the start of a process of negotiation. In doing so, a Works Council often creates an 'us against them' dynamics and this is perfectly in place in a more individualist society with low power distance. But it is not suitable for the dominantly collectivist and hierarchical culture in Angola, in which contradiction and confrontation is avoided and opposing leadership is frowned upon or outright rejected.

We did not want to organize opposition and we also suspected it would not work that way. What we sought to create was a formal space to invite the front workers to speak their minds in the harmonious manner which we had observed in our cultural environment. The fact that they carried, at least informally, the title of Soba, added to their possibility to do so.

The Chairman of the Council had indeed been hesitant for this same reason: "At first, I questioned myself whether I should accept to participate in the meetings because I thought it was about the creation of a union council. (...) Union councils around here tend to be very radical in terms of the demands from employers." Far more than organizing demands and institutionalizing bargaining power, therefore, the Soba Council created space for open, yet very respectful and harmonious dialogue. In Chapter 4, the various 'traditional' spaces were mentioned, where people are invited to contribute: courts, kgotla's, councils, and extended family gatherings under numerous different names and all over the continent. A small example was added in Chapter 5, with the account of the marriage proceedings that Silva witnessed. The Council could probably rather be compared to these fora: specific, formal gatherings in which the people with less power and seniority may also be invited to speak, albeit temporarily and usually only within that space. The practice of the Council, therefore, is probably closer to this Angolan tradition than to Portuguese management practice. It can be considered a transplant of such a formal space for dialogue, found within the Angolan governance and family systems in contemporary traditional fashion, into a privately owned business with a Portuguese management team. This transplant forms the biggest innovation from both Angolan and Portuguese perspectives.

For Silva and his management team, there were other significant differences between a Works Council and the Culture Council as well.

A Works Council bypasses two other important functions that we were hoping the Culture Council could play. It was to be (and turned out to be) a culture-informative body to bridge the gap between Portuguese management and the Angolan frontliners' cultural environment. The last ones were able to explain some of their cultural traits as well as react to our proposals or questions according to their own intrinsic values.

Within this aspect, the name Culture Council comes into its own; cultural exchange is one of the objectives. In itself this function changes both narratives. Or rather it doesn't change them in their core, but it adds a recurring theme to the dialogue, to bridge the gaps between peoples from at least two different nations and continents.

A third difference is that usually in a Works Council the two parties talk and negotiate, after which everybody goes his or her way. The people around the table do get to know each other and naturally some relationship building takes place, yet the rationale is to functionally systematize communication channels. In the case of the Culture Council, there is deliberate emphasis on relationship building for its own sake. It was meant for the participants to be together, to share experiences and sometimes a meal, and to get to know each other at a personal level.

In this respect, the biggest adaptation comes from the 'western' narrative of a Works Council, and what is considered correct professional forms of interaction in the West. It is the influence of the Angolan narrative and obviously one can point at collectivism, or, as Metz puts it: "one particular interpretation of African tradition, which treats harmonious and communal relationship as an end."[4]

The Chairman of the Council, from his perspective, added a fourth difference between the Culture Council and a Works or Union Council. Apart from the 'radical demands' mentioned above, when asked for the difference between the Culture Council and a Union Council, he answered as follows: "A Union Council is easily corrupted representing the interests of a minority in leadership rather than the collective of grassroots workers. (…) In the Culture Council the seven members aimed to create a healthy and wholesome environment between employees of different ranks and their families. We also aimed to create a direct link between the grassroots employee and the company management without the undue exclusions that exist in many institutions. We also aimed to highlight the achievements of employees throughout the year at a get-together dinner with all employees and their immediate family. At these galas, the members were ineligible, regardless of their achievements during the year, so we focused on the interests and achievements of the employees and not of ourselves."

Hence, in his experience, a Works or Union Council is often accepted ceremoniously, providing space for a minority to take care of itself. The Culture Council, however, was cut from a different cloth and acted in line with the community guidelines and leadership integrity, as found during the cultural research described in Chapters 4 and 5.

In other words, the Culture/Soba Council that was created was a completely different form than the Works or Union Council that either Silva knew from Portugal, or the Chairman knew from Angola. Since deeper cultural values are only detectable through inference, it is impossible to create a direct causality, but at least it is safe to conclude that

[4] Metz (2022, p. 8).

they worked in line with the common cultural ground they had. Both came from a tender culture, where humility and consensus seeking are of high value; and both come from a short-term oriented culture, with high respect for traditional wisdom and institutions. Both saw the purpose of the Council as well as their role therein as very distinct and together they created something new. In the words of Silva:

A Works Council would completely bypass our goal to create a company-wide solution, pulling people together rather than pushing people apart. In short, the Culture Council was meant to be far more inclusive, open minded, and harmonious, giving a voice as well as asking commitment, both from employees and from management. Instead of an 'us against them' mentality, this Council created the conditions for 'together we will rise.'

African Leadership

In the previous chapter, Silva mentioned that he observed new leadership skills emerging among the Council members. Within these slowly emerging new leadership roles, the young leaders still had (mostly) foreign managers above them within the organization. Moreover, these foreign managers were Portuguese, i.e. their former colonizer and we've seen that these relations are far from equal. In that sense it should be noted that the answer to the question "Can the Subaltern Speak,"[5] i.e. has it been possible for the less powerful to find an authentic voice, can only be answered partially: the Angolan frontliners have taken up more space than before (among them two women), they have found a voice and have been influential, but they cannot be called completely independent. Still, these new representatives took the lead in the midst of their co-workers, and management had to deal with a new reality as well. In this paragraph, the question is posed what the performative elements were concerning African leadership.

The history of the African continent, with both clashes and confluence of cultures taking place, has brought about new chances as well as possible pitfalls for African leadership. To start with the last, everybody is aware of the corruption, repression, and dictatorship that the continent has witnessed and is still witnessing today. Jallow talks of 'dark leadership'

[5] Spivak (1988; see Chapter 3 of this book).

in this respect, and he argues that "the colonial state lives on in post-colonial Africa."[6] In full, this dark leadership has probably been produced by a toxic combination of the colonial legacy, some of the traditional forms of authority and the fact that communal (local) checks & balances were not up to the task to check the authority exerted at a (foreign created) national level. In their book on African leadership, Jordans and others confirm that their research in several African countries "reveals that leadership practices in Africa are indeed a hybrid form of traditional leadership practices, colonial influences, and leadership practices that have been impacted by Western concepts and frameworks of leadership."[7]

The same ingredients have brought forth examples of 'bright leadership' as well, with shining examples like Nelson Mandela in South Africa, or Ellen Johnson Sirleaf of Liberia.[8] Jordans adds Seretse Khama of Botswana to this illustrious list, and of course such examples of bright leadership do not only occur at national political level with the spotlights of the world on them. They can be found at various levels as well as in little corners of society.[9]

Jordans[10] formulates three characteristics or dimensions of African leadership, which are based on deeply rooted values around good leadership:

1. Community: collectivism and 'doing good' as a very important feature.
2. Hierarchy: authority (power distance) and transformational leadership; leading the way.
3. Humane orientation: people-oriented leadership; integrity and servant leadership.

The challenge lies in the balancing act between those characteristics within the modern context. Looking at the Soba Council, with employees

[6] Jallow (2014, p. 8).

[7] Jordans et al. (2020, p. 321).

[8] Jallow (2014).

[9] It is too early to classify the recent wave of military coups in West-Africa into these two categories, caused by a mix of international jihadism, climate change, poverty, anti-neo-colonialism and a revolutionary youth.

[10] Jordans et al. (2020, p. 47).

taking up a new leadership role, we see both the first and the third characteristics, Community and Humane orientation, clearly featuring. In Chapter 6, the Chairman was cited, addressing the company during the Annual Company Ceremony, and urging his colleagues to look at them as their representatives: all employees could use them as their channel towards management and the Council existed to support the company for the good of all, as a form of servant leadership. On top, with the choice for a humanitarian activity for a rural community, as well as by asking respite for the laid off employee, the Council exhibited its felt responsibility for 'doing good'.

It is possible to observe most evolution, or "creative adaptation,"[11] as Iwowo calls it, in the second characteristic: Hierarchy. Up to four aspects of innovation concerning hierarchy can be detected in the newly established Soba Council and, as is only natural when innovation takes place, the frontliners showed some hesitation in their adoption. The first is the adoption of the Council meeting as one of these spaces where relative free speech is being allowed and even asked for, which meant they would try to speak freely in the presence of the Country Director and other managers. In chapter 6 one of the members was cited, saying that "Overcoming shyness and apathy towards the hierarchical superior," had been very challenging. The acceptance of, and the enactment of the behaviour that belongs to, the traditional open spaces within a modern business context points towards the open ended, performative nature of this tradition.

Secondly, the traditional respect for old age shifted slightly in this case study: the notion that age determines hierarchical role and that a title like Soba could hardly be given to a younger person. Most members of the Council were quite young and indeed they were reluctant to carry this title all the way. Yet, eventually they also got used to it, were inspired by it and some of them embraced it fully. All in all, the title gave direction to the behaviour of the Council members.

Thirdly, it is important to notice that two of the members of the Soba Council were female. Even though matrilineality is common among Bantu peoples (among whom the Mbundu of Luanda), and despite illustrious women like the Queen of Ndongo and Matamba (1581–1663) as one of the strongest female leaders and role models in Angola up

[11] Iwowo (2015, p. 420).

to today,[12] there have not been many female Sobas in Angolan history. In this case, two young women were selected member of the Culture Council and consequently, were regularly called Soba, along with the others.

Finally, the frontliners had to think deeply what to do with their succession, as traditional leadership often lasts a lifetime. Only after a lot of discussion and reflection, taking place over at least two Council meetings, they decided it is wise to step down and clear the way for others. In doing so they created flexibility in hierarchical roles; power remained with the role and not with the person, which implies a movement from ascribed leadership into the direction of achieved leadership.

These experiences portray the flexibility of the concept of the Soba, highlighting a form of 'bright leadership,' which can be used in a variety of contexts. The concept exhibits elements of continuity in relation to the past, the present, and the future and can be applied to create new meaning. In conclusion, the performative nature within the theme of African leadership in this case study, or one could say, most of the "invention of tradition,"[13] is found in the essence and the level of accepted and enacted hierarchy. This finding falls in tune with the research of Jordans (et al.), who found a widespread desire for lower enactment of hierarchy in several African countries, striving for a newly emerging balance. They found the inception of a new generation of leaders: the young generation is both asking for more transparency and good governance as well as taking the lead and leading by example.[14]

Western Leadership in Africa

While the story of Silva and the Culture Council reveals interesting lessons for internal organizational dialogue, community building and African leadership, it also holds some good recommendations for the Western leader, doing business on the African continent and for geocentric leadership in general. Throughout this book, it has been argued that in leadership style, the 'one size fits all' practices don't transfer well between different cultures. What is expected of a 'good leader' differs widely across

[12] For a comic strip from Unesco, see Joubeaud et al. (2014).

[13] Eze (2010, p. 2).

[14] Jordans et al. (2020).

the globe. Therefore, it also demands quite some adaptation from a leader who is travelling the world and enacting leadership in a different country than his/her own.

For a subsidiary from a foreign country, ignorance of culture sensitive preferences for leadership can easily result in misunderstandings, tensions, and low employee satisfaction, motivation, and commitment. In case a company from one country opens a subsidiary in another country, the form of leadership that is being executed should at least be explained extensively to prevent misinterpretation and should at certain instances reflect local preferences, customs, and habits.

In this particular case, the challenge for Silva to create meaningful dialogue was threefold. He needed to cross the racial and old colonial power structure that is still largely intact, as Åkesson has shown.[15] Furthermore, he needed to bridge the difference between Portuguese and Angolan cultural values of power distance. On top, he needed to bridge the fact that he was the Country Director while he longed to speak and especially listen to his subordinates in the context of this subsidiary. The most important performative, cultural adaptation from the Portuguese side, therefore, was the strive to forge community within a foreign company structure and to develop much stronger, personal relationships between himself as the Country Director and his management team on the one hand, and the Angolan employees on the other.

Overall, Western organizations in individualist societies do have a hard time and/or need special measures to mobilize effort and to inspire people to go above and beyond. When it comes to mobilizing human capability, it is communities that tie individuals together and which easily outperform mechanical bureaucracies. Communities depend on common norms, values, and the gentle prodding of one's peers. Within communities, capability and disposition are naturally imposed and involvement is mostly at an emotional level. Employees exercise their talents partly voluntarily, in return for the chance to make a difference for the whole group. When compared with bureaucracies, communities tend to look undermanaged. That, more than anything else, is why they are amplifiers of human capabilities and may have exponential impact. In a community you are 'partners in crime' and commitment is based on one's affiliation with the group's aims and goals. A

[15] Åkesson (2018).

strong corporate culture based on this solidarity is generally like a normative glue, that holds the dynamic behaviour of an organization.

Apart from the fact that the Country Director had a company to run and needed to think about input, operations and clients, it took time investment, relationship building, but above all a genuine interest in and respect for the employees, and for the people and culture of Angola. Not surprisingly, Metz writes: "One interesting implication of building communal relationships in the workplace concerns the role of emotions. By the relational moral theory, cultivating certain feelings and attitudes merits doing so as an end, not merely as a means in order, say, to motivate employees to perform. A communal or harmonious relationship is not merely a matter of coordination and aid, but also includes emotional aspects. For one, part of identifying with others involves a sense of togetherness such as feeling pride in what others accomplish and liking being with them, and for another, exhibiting solidarity with others includes feeling sympathy and compassion. In so far as one major of a business leader is to foster communality in a firm, (s)he must be committed to prompting such feelings and attitudes."[16] It is this pride in what others accomplish, enjoying being with them, and having feelings of empathy, compassion and solidarity, which are very clear from the accounts of Silva, especially found in Chapters 6 and 7.

Within a geocentric approach, leaders are not only aware of these challenges, but it also places a high demand on the capabilities and mindset of a true global leader. According to Gupta, a true geocentric leader should have a highly complex cognitive structure characterized by an openness to and articulation of multiple cultural and strategic realities on both global and local levels, and the cognitive ability to mediate and integrate across this multiplicity.[17] In our case, this is probably true both for Silva and for the Chairman of the Soba Council, while they were steering the process of transformative change together. In the case of the Culture/Soba Council, one adaptation for all parties was the increased complexity of dialogue and negotiations, as information and demands could now come from different directions. The line of command for all, from Country Director to the management team, all the way down to the members of the Council, had become more complex and more integrated.

[16] Metz (2022, p. 219).

[17] Gupta and Govindarajan (2002).

The effort to be more of a geocentric leader is a demanding task and just 'having an open mind' is not enough. It takes deep awareness of one's own cultural programming; the continuous search and analyses of the content of the cultural differences; and the translation of these into a workable organization, strategy, policies, and procedures.

Geocentric HR

Conclusions have been drawn so far, situating this case study in the greater story of complementarity and confluence of cultures and concluding on the harmonious dialogue that was created in the Culture Council, creating room for cultural exchange, relationship building, and striving for the common good according to community guidelines. Before Silva will make some final remarks at the end of this chapter, he looks back from a manager's point of view on the implications for the Human Resources departments of MNC's.

It was observed that international assignments have quite a large chance of failure and I also realized that my deployment to Angola had been more challenging than I had expected. The work on international assignments, therefore, is highly demanding for HR departments at the headquarters of MNCs and should be initiated long before an assignee arrives to the host country.[18] *To avoid the costly failure of home country staff in international assignments, it is important to select the 'right' employees and it is a wise thing to pay attention to cultural competence and flexibility in the selection process. It may start with a pre-program assessment and exploration, including an evaluation of the expatriates and family member's background, such as host culture, personal tendencies, and prior international experience.*

Prior experience is not necessarily an advantage though: one study has shown that expatriates are exhibiting higher levels of adjustment during their first international assignment, becoming less flexible at successive stations.[19] Learning and adjusting to another culture prove to take an immense amount of energy and resilience; many people will not be able to do this frequently in their lives.

[18] Brislin and Yoshida (1993).

[19] Stahl (1998).

After selection, these employees and their families would need the proper cross-cultural preparation, support, and training. The company can perform an expatriate and family training program to increase the assignee's knowledge about the host country, including values, customs, behaviours, business culture, and day-to-day living. The preparation procedure can be finalized by arranging a cultural briefing with the host team with which the expatriate will be working, fostering the identification of different styles of management, expectations, and communication. Future interactions with the expatriates can also be performed with project alignment meetings, in-country coaching as the assignment is being developed, including a knowledge management process with the capture of know-how and experience.

Experience of the authors shows that cultural training and/or coaching often needs to continue after the employee and his/her family have spent some time in the host country. Having experienced different cultural occurrences by that time (sometimes clashes or even shocks), the cultural knowledge now falls into far more fertile soil and at that point it is much better understood, appreciated, and can be made immediately applicable to their specific context. As Silva mentioned earlier, cultural differences call for a lifelong learning journey. It is the power of repetition, further application in new contexts, situations, and circumstances, possibly together with local managers and staff getting the chance to explain their part of reality in a culturally sensitive manner, which will lead to the cultural competence needed of a true geocentric leader.

Apart from a thorough selection, preparation, and continued support, keeping a finger firmly on the pulse from HR at HQ, it is important to mention briefly, that the HR policies within the subsidiaries abroad would need adaptation in many of its rules and regulations as well. An ethnocentric approach can jeopardize a company's ability to attract, retain, and leverage its pool of local talent. Cultural aspects deeply influence the employee's motivation, job satisfaction, and commitment to the company. Furthermore, decision-making processes, conflict resolution, and performance appraisals differ widely across cultures.

It has become clear that personal relationship between superior and subordinate is a very important motivator on the African continent, compared to the west. In addition, the list of additional parameters, that should rather not be managed assuming only the western standards, is long. For instance, one should think about recruitment (via networks); training (long term apprenticeship); discipline (lead by example and being one's brother's keeper); motivation (relationships; and loyalty and security).[20]

At the same time, this story serves as a testament that it is frequently necessary to go way beyond training and coaching of foreign managers and their families, and beyond the realm of HR, in order to create competitive advantage. In those cases, cultural management finds its place at the strategy table of management, for them to gear and embark on a cultural change process. This is both true for management of the subsidiary as well as at HQ.

For the MNC as a whole, it is the geocentric approach which enables the establishment of permissible local standards variation, ensuring the adoption of practices that enable the achievement of the company goals. To increase control and global coordination, HQ may establish a set of guidelines (rather than standards) mainly in functions such as finance, strategy and product development. The establishment of worldwide guidelines and permissible local standards should balance between what effectively works in the company headquarter and subsidiary, fostering a collaborative network between both.[21]

Final Remarks

In conclusion, the story of the creation of a Culture Council within a Portuguese subsidiary in Angola forms an interesting case study, in which confluence of different cultural narratives takes place. The story describes the transformative change process, creating an invented tradition in the form of a Culture Council, with the partially accepted name of Soba Council, as a new space for dialogue between frontliners and management within a foreign private business. The main performative adaptations on the Angolan side were found in the acceptance of the Council as a space to speak up towards management, and in the hierarchical features of the original Soba leader: the new Soba's were young, two of them were female and the power stayed with the role rather than with the person, after succession. On the Portuguese side, the management team had to move from a task-based, rather nonpersonal bureaucratic organization, towards the forging of personal relationships and community.

[20] See Iguisi (2014), Iguisi and Hofstede (1993), Jackson (2004), and Dia (1996).

[21] Gupta and Govindarajan (2002).

As a final remark, I can state that our company successfully managed to optimally balance the advantages of a good interaction with the headquarters office for aggregating know-how and coordinating activities on the one hand, with the advantages of making use of local know-how, involving our employees in all company activities and encouraging the flow of information bottom-up and top-down on the other.

In collectivist societies, the ingredients of community and a strong company culture are available and abundant yet remain often unused. Of course, it takes time, effort, and authentic interest to study them and to find innovative ways of merging them with the standing organization. In our case, both the Hofstede model with its 6 dimensions, as well as Genchi Genbutsu from the Toyota way, were very suitable tools for analysis and understanding. Cultural difference is never easy and often leads to misunderstanding, frustration, even bitterness. Yet the Hofstede model explained unconscious patterns that none of us could have suspected, and formulated these in a neutral vocabulary, leading us to deep insight. Genchi Genbutsu provided us with the opportunity to find positively formulated cultural adaptors and concepts, which could be used in an innovative way within organizational change.

Apart from time and innovative energy, it is true that the implementation entails a higher degree of leadership complexity, due to multiple cultural and strategic realities on both global and local levels. Having to deal with today's conditions of rapid change and uncertainty is a daunting task in itself and here we are adding another level of complication. Yet, I believe this is a question of the company and leader's deliberate choice. Without it, there are many companies that keep afloat for quite some time, dependent on the competitiveness of their markets. Still, they lose out on a day-to-day basis and, on top, there is a high probability that they will experience painful events and surprises.

This could be prevented by trying to approach geocentric leadership: be more comfortable with other peoples and cultures; strive for the bigger; broader picture; accept life as a balance of contradictory forces; trust organizational processes rather than structure; and value diversity. As Nelson Mandela once mentioned: "If you want the cooperation of humans around you, you must make them feel they are important - and you do that by being genuine and humble."[22]

[22] Mandela in Profit Magazin (2013).

I want to express my deepest gratitude to all the Culture/ Soba Council members for the courage "one-for-all" and service "above-self," demonstrated when embracing this incredible transformative journey. Your effort and dedication to the task at hand have not gone unnoticed and I truly believe that our work alongside had an undoubtedly very positive impact on our company performance. My sincere admiration and respect for all your invaluable contributions. Many thanks to all from the bottom of my heart!

References

Åkesson, L. (2018). *Postcolonial Portuguese migration to Angola*. Palgrave Macmillan.

Beugelsdijk, S., & Welzel, C. (2018). Dimensions and dynamics of national culture: Synthesizing Hofstede with Inglehart. *Journal of Cross-Cultural Psychology, 49*(10), 1469–1505.

Brislin, R. W., & Yoshida, T. (1993). *Improving intercultural interactions: Models for cross-cultural training programs*. Sage.

Dia, M. (1996). *Africa's management in the 1990's and beyond: Reconciling indigenous and transplanted institutions*. The International Bank for Reconstruction and Development, The World Bank.

Eze, M. O. (2010). *Intellectual history in contemporary South Africa*. Palgrave Macmillan.

Geschiere, P., Meyer, B., & Pels, P. (Eds.). (2009). *Readings in modernity in Africa*. Indiana University Press.

Gupta, A. K., & Govindarajan, V. (2002). Cultivating a global mindset. *The Academy of Management Executive, 16*(1), 116–126.

Hofstede, G., Hofstede, G. J., & Minkov, M. (2010). *Cultures and organizations: Software of the mind*. McGraw-Hill.

Hofstede, G. J. (2019). *BOSS Blog 1: Do cultures change?* https://geerthofstede.com/boss-blog-1-do-cultures-change/. Consulted on 12 August 2020.

Iguisi, O., & Hofstede, G. (1993). *Industrial management in an African culture*. IRIC University of Limburg Press.

Iguisi, O. (2014). African values for the practice of HRM. *Beykent University Journal of Social Sciences, 7*(1), 56–77.

Iwowo, V. (2015). Leadership in Africa: Rethinking development. *Personnel Review, 44*(3), 408–429.

Jackson, T. (2004). *Management and change in Africa: A cross-cultural perspective*. Routledge.

Jallow, B. G. (2014). Leadership in colonial Africa: An Introduction. In B. Jallow (Ed.), *Leadership in postcolonial Africa: Trends transformed by independence*. Palgrave Macmillan.

Jordans, E., Ng'wena, B., & Spencer-Oatey, H. (Eds.). (2020). *Developing global leaders: Insights from African case studies.* Palgrave Macmillan.

Joubeaud, E., Masioni, P., & Serbin, S. (2014). *Njinga Mbandi: Queen of Ndondo and Matanga.* Comic strip of the United Nations Educational, Scientific and Cultural Organization. https://unesdoc.unesco.org/ark:/48223/pf0000230103. Consulted on 15 February 2023.

Kirkman, B. L., Lowe, K. B., & Gibson, C. B. (2006). A quarter century of 'culture's consequences': A review of empirical research incorporating Hofstede's cultural values framework. *Journal of International Business Studies, 37*, 285–320.

Mandela, N. (2013). Interview with Oprah Winfrey. *Profitmagazin 63/64.*

Metz, T. (2022). *A relational moral theory: African ethics in and beyond the continent.* Oxford University Press.

Spivak, G. C. (1988). Can the subaltern speak? In C. Nelson & L. Grossberg (Eds.), *Marxism and the interpretation of culture* (pp. 271–313). Macmillan.

Stahl, G. K. (1998). *Internationaler Einsatz von Führungskräften.* München, Germany.

Epilogue: Navigating the Space of Cultural Confluence

As the journey of Silva through the implementation of a culture-specific change process is accomplished, the crossroads of individual understanding leads to further inspiration and action. In fact, the chapters of this book have woven together a rich narrative of perspectives, principles, methods, and strategies that empower organizational practitioners, managers, and businesspeople to navigate novel management approaches.

In the digital era, the oceans for readers engagement have expanded exponentially, connecting global audiences in an unprecedented way. Therefore, an official website of the book was created: www.spacesofconfluence.com, with the objective of adding additional resources for further reading, including a "space" for sharing case studies and other useful items. The "Space of Cultural Confluence" website is a living resource, a breathing extension of this book, empowering the path towards a more vibrant, inclusive, and culturally enriched world.

You are invited to gain more insight, read more stories, but also to share your own story on cultural confluence! Whether large or tiny, all embracing or seemingly insignificant: cultural confluence happens continuously where people care to listen and act together. Please share your story!

A. Vonk and V. F. Silva, *Cultural Confluence in Organizational Change*, Palgrave Studies in African Leadership,
https://doi.org/10.1007/978-3-031-45403-5

Bibliography

Achebe, C. (1958). *Things fall apart*. William Heinemann Ltd.

Ahluwalia, P. (2001). *Politics and post-colonial theory: African inflections*. Routledge.

Ailon, G. (2008). Mirror, mirror on the wall: Culture's consequences in a value test of its own design. *Academy of Management Review, 33*, 885–904.

Alcock, G. G. (2015). *Kasinomics*. Tracey McDonald Publishers.

Alcock, G. G. (2018). *Kasinomics revolution*. Tracey McDonald Publishers.

Appiah, K. A. (2006). *Cosmopolitanism: Ethics in a world of strangers*. Allen Lane.

Awori, T. (2022). *Leadership in Africa redefined*. Action Wealth Publishing.

Åkesson, L. (2018). *Postcolonial Portuguese migration to Angola*. Palgrave Macmillan.

Ball, D. A., McCulloch, Jr., W. H., Frantz, P. L., Geringer, J. M., & Minor, M. S. (2004). *International business: The challenges of global competition* (9th ed.). McGraw-Hill Irwin.

Banerjee, S. B. (2000). Whose land is it anyway? National interest, indigenous stakeholders, and colonial discourses. *Organization and the Environment, 13*(4), 3–38.

Bartlett, C. A., & Ghoshal, S. (1989). *Managing across boarders: The transnational solution*. Harvard Business School Press.

Barlett et al. (2008). *Transnational management: Text, cases and readings in cross-border management* (5th ed.). McGraw-Hill.

Battle, M. (1996). The ubuntu theology of Desmond Tutu. In I. Hulley, L. Kretzchmar, & L. L. Pato (Eds.), *Archbishop Tutu: Prophetic witness in South Africa* (pp. 93–105). Human & Rousseau.

A. Vonk and V. F. Silva, *Cultural Confluence in Organizational Change*, Palgrave Studies in African Leadership,
https://doi.org/10.1007/978-3-031-45403-5

Bennett, J. M., & Bennett, M. J. (2002). *Intercultural communication for practitioners*. Zürich University Press.

Bennett, M. J. (2017). Constructivist approach to intercultural communication. In Y. Kim (Ed.), *International encyclopedia of intercultural communication*. Wiley.

Beugelsdijk, S., Maseland, R., & van Hoorn, A. (2015). Are scores on Hofstede's dimensions of national culture stable over time? A cohort analysis. In *Global Strategy Journal, 5,* 223–240.

Beugelsdijk, S., & Welzel, C. (2018). Dimensions and dynamics of national culture: Synthesizing Hofstede with Inglehart. *Journal of Cross-Cultural Psychology, 49*(10), 1469–1505.

Bhengu, M. J. (2011). *African economic humanism: The rise of an African economic philosophy.* Gowing Publishing Limited.

Boubakri, N., Guedhami, O., Kwok, C. C. Y., & Safar, W. (2016). National culture and privatization: The relationship between collectivism and residual state ownership. *Journal of International Business Studies, 47*, 170–190.

Brislin, R. W., & Yoshida, T. (1993). *Improving intercultural interactions: Models for cross-cultural training programs.* Sage.

Cabrera, A., & Unruh, G. (2012). *Being global: How to think, act and lead in a transformed world*. Harvard Business Review Press.

Candido, M. (2013). *An African slaving port and the Atlantic World: Benguela and its hinterland*. Cambridge University Press.

Césaire, A. (2001). *Discourse on colonialism.* New York University Press. (*Discours sur le colonialism, orig.* 1950).

Chinese Culture Connection. (1987). Chinese values and the search for culture-free dimensions of culture. *Journal of Cross-Cult: Psychology, 18*(2), 143–164.

Dalai Lama. (2010). *Toward a true kinship of faiths: How the world's religions can come together*. Three Rivers Press.

Dandala, M. (2009). Cows never die: Embracing African cosmology in the process of economic growth. In M. F. Murove (Ed.), *African ethics: An anthology of comparative and applied ethics* (pp. 259–277). KwaZulu-Natal Press.

Deresky, H. (2007). *A review of international management: Managing across borders and cultures* (6th ed.). Pearson Prentice Hall.

De Witte, M. (2012). Buy the future now! Charismatic chronotypes in neo-liberal Ghana. *Etnofoor, 24*(1), 80–104.

Dia, M. (1996). *Africa's management in the 1990's and beyond: Reconciling indigenous and transplanted institutions.* The International Bank for Reconstruction and Development, The World Bank.

Drogendijk, R., & Slangen, A. (2006). Hofstede, Schwartz, or managerial perceptions? The effects of different cultural distance measures on establishment mode choices by multinational enterprises. *International Business Review, 15*, 361–380.

Ekeh, P. P. (1975). Colonialism and the two publics in Africa: A theoretical statement. *Comparative Studies in Society and History, 17*(1), 91–112.

Eze, C. (2014). Rethinking African culture and identity: The Afropolitan model. *Journal of African Cultural Studies, 26*(2), 234–247.

Eze, M. O. (2010). *Intellectual history in contemporary South Africa*. Palgrave Macmillan.

Eze, M. O. (2022). Interculturality as dialogical reciprocity in African and comparative philosophy. *Filosofie & Praktijk, 43*(3/4), 49–64.

Eze, M. O., & Van der Wal, K. (2020). Beyond sovereign reason: Issues and contestations in contemporary African identity. *Journal of Common Market Studies, 58*(1), 189–205.

Fanon, F. (1967). First truths on the colonial problem. *Toward the African Revolution* (H. Chevalier, Trans.). Penguin.

Fanon, F. (1968). *On national culture and the pitfalls of national consciousness. The wretched of the earth* (C. Farrington, Trans.). Grove Press.

Fanon, F. (1990). *The wretched of the earth* (Third Translation, C. Farrington, Trans.). Penguin.

Finuras, P. (2013). *Cultural values and trust in institutions: A comparative study between Portugal, Angola, Cape Verde Islands and Mozambique* (Doctoral Research.). Luso University Lisbon.

Finuras, P. (2014). *Em Quem Confiamos? Valores culturais e (des)confiança nas instituições*. Edições Sílabo.

Fischer, R., Vauclair, M. C., Fontaine, J. R. J., & Schwartz, S. H. (2010). Are individual-level and country-level value structures different? Testing Hofstede's legacy with the Schwartz value survey. *Journal of Cross-Cultural Psychology, 41*(2), 135–151.

Friedman, T. L. (2005). *The world is flat*. Farrar, Straus and Giroux.

Geschiere, P., Meyer, B., & Pels, P. (Eds.). (2009). *Readings in modernity in Africa*. Indiana University Press.

Ghemawat, P. (2001, September). Distance still matters. *Harvard Business Review, 79*(8), 1–11.

Ghemawat, P. (2009). Why the world isn't flat. *Foreign Policy*. https://foreignpolicy.com/2009/10/14/why-the-world-isnt-flat. Consulted on 29 October 2019.

Gikandi, S. (2010). Foreword: On Afropolitanism. In J. Wawrzinek & J. K. S. Makokha (Eds.), *Negotiating Afropolitanism: Essays on borders and spaces in contemporary African literature and Folklore* (pp. 9–11). Rodopi.

Graness, A. (2016). Writing the history of philosophy in Africa: Where to begin? *Journal of African Cultural Studies, 28*(2), 132–146. https://doi.org/10.1080/13696815.2015.1053799

Gupta, A. K., & Govindarajan, V. (2002). Cultivating a global mindset. *The Academy of Management Executive, 16*(1), 116–126.

Gyekye, K. (1997). *Tradition and modernity: Philosophical reflections on the African experience*. Oxford University Press.

Gyekye, K. (2004). *The unexamined life: Philosophy and the African experience*. Sankofa Publishing Company.

Hall, E., & Reed Hall, M. (1990). *Understanding cultural differences*. Intercultural Press.

Hall, S. (1994). Cultural identity and diaspora. In P. Williams & L. Chrisman (Eds.), *Colonial discourse and postcolonial theory: A reader* (pp. 392–403). Columbia University Press.

Hamel, G. (2007). *The future of management*. Harvard Business School Press.

Hill, C. W. L. (2005). *International business: Competing in the global marketplace* (5th ed.). McGraw-Hill Irwin.

Hochberg, N., Klick, J., & Reilly, E. (2015, September 16). What companies have learned from losing billions in emerging markets. *Harvard Business Review*. https://hbr.org/2015/09/what-companies-have-learned-from-losing-billions-in-emerging-markets. Consulted on 5 October 2019.

Hodgetts, R. M., & Luthans, F. (2003). *International management: Culture, strategy and behaviour* (5th ed.). McGraw-Hill Irwin.

Hofstede, G. (1980a). *Culture's consequences: International differences in work-related values*. Sage.

Hofstede, G. (1980b). Motivation, leadership, and organization: Do American theories apply abroad? *Organizational Dynamics, 9*, 42–63.

Hofstede, G. (1993). Cultural constraints in management theories. *The Executive, 7*(1), 81–94.

Hofstede, G. (1998). *Masculinity and femininity: The taboo dimensions of national cultures*. Sage.

Hofstede, G. (2001). *Culture's consequences: Comparing values, behaviors, institutions and organizations across nations* (2nd ed.). Sage.

Hofstede, G. (2002). Dimensions do not exist: A reply to Brendan McSweeney. *Human Relations, 55*(11), 1355–1361.

Hofstede, G., Hofstede, G. J., & Minkov, M. (2010). *Cultures and organizations: Software of the mind*. McGraw-Hill.

Hofstede, G. J. (2019). *BOSS Blog 1: Do cultures change?* https://geerthofstede.com/boss-blog-1-do-cultures-change/. Consulted on 12 August 2020.

Holtbrügge, D. (2022). *Intercultural management: Concepts, practice, critical reflection*. Sage.

Horwitz, F. M., Cook, F. L., & Kamoche, K. (2021). Human resource management in emerging markets: Theoretical perspectives for understanding contexts. In E. Parry, J. M. Michael, & C. Brewster (Eds.), *The Oxford handbook of contextual approaches to human resource management*. https://doi.org/10.1093/oxfordhb/9780190861162.013.6

Horwitz, F. M., Kamoche, K., & Chew, I. K. H. (2002). Human resource management in Africa. *International Journal of Human Resource Management, 13*(7), 1019–1041.

House, R. J., Hanges, P. J., Javidan, M., Dorfman, P. W., & Gupta, V. (2004). *Culture, leadership, and organizations: The GLOBE study of 62 societies*. Sage.

Iguisi, O. (1994). Appropriate management in an African culture. *Journal of Management in Nigeria, 30*(1), 16–24.

Iguisi, O. (2014). African values for the practice of HRM. *Beykent University Journal of Social Sciences, 7*(1), 56–77.

Iguisi, O., & Hofstede, G. (1993). *Industrial management in an African culture*. IRIC University of Limburg Press.

Inglehart, R., & Baker, W. E. (2000). Modernization, cultural change, and the persistence of traditional values. *American Sociological Review, 65*(1), 19–51.

Iwowo, V. (2015). Leadership in Africa: Rethinking development. *Personnel Review, 44*(3), 408–429.

Jackson, T. (2004). *Management and change in Africa: A cross-cultural perspective*. Routledge.

Jallow, B. G. (2014a). The case for African leadership case studies and leadership in colonial Africa: An introduction. In B. Jallow (Ed.), *Leadership in colonial Africa: Disruption of traditional frameworks and patterns*. Palgrave Macmillan.

Jallow, B. G. (2014b). Leadership in colonial Africa: An introduction. In B. Jallow (Ed.), *Leadership in postcolonial Africa: Trends transformed by independence*. Palgrave Macmillan.

Jayaram, K., Sanghvi, S., & Riese, J. (2010, June). *Africa's path to growth, sector by sector*. McKinsey and Company. https://www.mckinsey.com/featured-insights/middle-east-and-africa/africas-path-to-growth-sector-by-sector. Consulted on 5 October 2019.

Jerónimo, M. B. (2015). *The 'civilising mission' of Portuguese colonialism 1870–1930*. Palgrave Macmillan.

Jordans, E., Ng'wena, B., & Spencer-Oatey, H. (Eds.). (2020). *Developing global leaders: Insights from African case studies*. Palgrave Macmillan.

Joubeaud, E., Masioni, P., & Serbin, S. (2014). *Njinga Mbandi: Queen of Ndondo and Matanga*. Comic strip of the United Nations Educational, Scientific and Cultural Organization. https://unesdoc.unesco.org/ark:/48223/pf0000230103. Consulted on 15 February 2023.

Khoza, R. (2006). *Let Africa lead: African transformational leadership for 21st century business*. Vezubuntu.

Kiggundu, M. N. (1991). The challenges of management development in Sub-Saharan Africa. *Journal of Management Development, 10*(6), 32–47.

Kirkman, B. L., Lowe, K. B., & Gibson, C. B. (2006). A quarter century of 'culture's consequences': A review of empirical research incorporating Hofstede's cultural values framework. *Journal of International Business Studies, 37*, 285–320.

Kirkman, B. L., Lowe, K. B., & Gibson, C. B. (2017). *A retrospective on cultures consequences: The 35-year journey*. https://api.research-repository.uwa.edu.au/ws/portalfiles/portal/24299027/Kirkman_et._al._2017_A_retrospective_on_Culture_s_Consequences.pdf. Consulted on 30 December 2022.

Kluckhohn, F. R., & Strodtbeck, F. I. (1961). *Variations in value orientation*. Evanston Univversity Press.

Kottak, C. (2006). *Mirror for humanity*. McGraw-Hill.

Kwek, D. (2003). Decolonizing and re-presenting culture's consequences: A postcolonial critique of cross-cultural studies in management. In A. Prasad (Ed.), *Postcolonial theory and organizational analysis* (pp. 121–148). Palgrave Macmillan.

Lanzer, F. (2017). *Leading across cultures in practice*. LCO Partners BV.

Lem, M., van Tulder, R., & Geleynse, K. (2013). *Doing business in Africa, a strategic guide for entrepreneurs*. Bereschot International B.V.; Partnerships Resource Centre at RSM Erasmus University Rotterdam and Netherlands-African Business Council.

Lessem, R., & Nussbaum, B. (1996). *Sawubona Africa: Embracing four worlds in South African management*. Zebra Press.

Liker, K. J. (2004). *The Toyota way: 14 management principles from the world's greatest manufacturer*. McGraw-Hill.

Lutz, D. (2009). African *Ubuntu* philosophy and global management. *Journal of Business Ethics, 84*, 313–328.

Magendane, K. (2020). Afrika na kolonialisatie: succesvol of mislukking? *Clingendael Spectator series on 60 years of independance*.

Malfense Fierro, A. C. (2015, July 31). After Obama comes the big challenge for Africa's entrepreneurs. *The Conversation*. https://theconversation.com/after-obama-comes-the-big-challenge-for-africas-entrepreneurs-45383. Consulted on 5 October 2019.

Mandela, N. (2013). Interview with Oprah Winfrey. *Profitmagazin 63/64*.

Mangaliso, M. P. (2001). Building a competitive advantage from ubuntu: Management lessons from South Africa. *The Academy of Management Executive, 15*(3), 23–33.

Marx, E. (2001). *Breaking through culture shock: What you need to succeed in international business*. Nicholas Brealey Publishers.

Mbeki, T. (1998). *Africa: The time has come*. Tafelberg.

Mbembe, A. (2007). Afropolitanism (L. Chauvet, Trans.). In S. Njami & L. Duran (Eds.), *African remix: Contemporary art of a continent* (pp. 26–29). Jacana Media.

Mbigi, L. (1997). *Ubuntu: The African dream in management*. Knowledge Resources.

Mbigi, L. (2000). *In search of the African business renaissance: An African cultural perspective*. Knowledge Resources.

Mbigi, L. (2005). *The spirit of African leadership*. Knowledge Resources.

Mbigi, L., & Maree, J. (1995). *The spirit of African transformation management*. Sigma.

Mbiti, J. S. (1969). *African religions & philosophy*. Heinemann.

McSweeney, B. (2002). Hofstede's model of national cultural differences and their consequences: A triumph of faith—A failure of analysis. *Human Relations, 55*, 89–118.

Meertens, J. V. (2017). *Do we have a deal? - Succesvol onderhandelen in andere culturen*. Zaltbommel, the Netherlands: Haystack.

Menkiti, I. A. (1984). African philosophy: An introduction. In R. A. Wright (Ed.), *Person and community in African traditional thought* (pp. 171–181). University Press of America.

Menkiti, I. A. (2006). On the normative conception of a person. In K. Wiredu (Ed.), *A companion to African philosophy* (pp. 324–331). Blackwell.

Metz, T. (2022). *A relational moral theory: African ethics in and beyond the continent*. Oxford University Press.

Meyer, E. (2014). *The culture map*. Public Affairs.

Minkov, M. (2007). *What makes us different and similar: A new interpretation of the world values survey and other cross-cultural data*. Klasika i Stil.

Minkov, M. (2014). *Cross-cultural analysis: The science and art of comparing the world's modern societies and their cultures*. Sage.

Minkov, M. (2018). A revision of Hofstede's model of national culture: Old evidence and new data from 56 countries. *Cross Cultural & Strategic Management, 25*(2), 231–256.

Minkov, M., & Kaasa, A. (2021). A test of the revised Minkov-Hofstede model of culture: Mirror images of subjective and objective culture across nations and the 50 US states. *Cross-Cultural Research, 55*(2–3), 230–281.

Minkov, M., & Kaasa, A. (2022). Do dimensions of culture exist objectively? A validation of the revised Minkov-Hofstede model of culture with world values survey items and scores for 102 countries. *Journal of International Management, 28*(4), 100791.

Minkov, M., Vignoles, V. L., Welzel, C., Akaliyski, P., Bond, M. H., Kaasa, A., & Smith, P. B. (2023, forthcoming). *Comparative culturology and cross-cultural psychology: How comparing societal cultures differs from comparing the minds of individuals across cultures*. See: https://www.youtube.com/watch?v=r74JmVwnmoM. Consulted on 27 October 2023.

Molose, T. (2019). The equivalence of Southern African heritage of Ubuntu. In H. H. Kazerooney, A. Stachowicz-Stanusch, & W. Amann (Eds.), *Advancing African knowledge management and education* (pp. 27–48). Information Age Publishing.

Mudimbe, V. Y. (1988). *The invention of Africa: Gnosis, philosophy, and the order of knowledge*. Indiana University Press.

Müller, L. (2023). Human wellbeing in intercultural philosophical perspective: A focus on the Akan philosophy of Wiredu, Gyekye, and Appiah. In B. Bateye, M. Masaeli, L. Müller, & A. Roothaan (Eds.), *Well-being in African philosophy: Insights for a global ethics of development* (pp. 13–49). Lexington Books by Rowman & Littlefield.

Nardal, J. (1929). Internationalisme noir. In S. B. Diagne (2010). Négritude. http://plato.stanford.edu/archives/spr2014/entries/negritude/. In E. N. Zalta (Ed.). (2014). *The Stanford encyclopedia of philosophy*.

Nardal, J. (2002). Black internationalism. In T. D. Sharpley-Whiting (Ed.), *Negritude women* (pp. 105–107). University of Minnesota Press.

Ndaba, W. J. (1994). *Ubuntu in comparison to western philosophies*. Ubuntu School of Philosophy.

Newenham-Kahindi, A. (2009). The transfer of Ubuntu and Indaba business models abroad: A case of South African multinational banks and telecommunication services in Tanzania. *International Journal of Cross-Cultural Management, 9*, 87–108.

Nkomo, S. M. (2011). A postcolonial and anti-colonial reading of 'African' leadership and management in organization studies: Tensions, contradictions and possibilities. *Organization, 18*(3), 365–386.

Nussbaum, B. (2003). Ubuntu: Reflections of a South African on our common humanity. *Reflections, 4*(4), 21–26.

Nyamnjoh, F. B. (2014). 'Our traditions are modern, our modernities traditional': Chieftancy and democracy in contemporary Cameroon and Botswana. *Modern Africa: Politics, History and Society, 2*(2), 13–62.

Osland, J., & Bird, A. (2006). Global leaders as experts. *Advances in Global Leadership, 4*, 125–145.

Perlmutter, H. (1969). The Tortuous evolution of multinational enterprises. *Columbia World Journal of Business, 4*(1), 9–18.

Perlmutter, V. H., & Heenan, A. D. (1974). How multinational should your top managers be? *Harvard Business Review, 52*(6), 1–13.

Reiter, B. (2021). The African origins of democracy. *Academia Letters*, Article 414. https://doi.org/10.20935/AL414

Schein, E. H. (1985). *Organizational culture and leadership*. Jossey-Bass Publishers.

Schneider, S., Barsoux, J. L., & Stahl, G. K. (2014). *Managing across cultures* (3rd ed.). Pearson Education Limited.

Schwartz, S. H. (1994). Beyond individualism/collectivism: New cultural dimensions of values. In U. Kim, C. Kagitcibasi, H. C. Triandis, S. C. Choi, & G. Yoon (Eds.), *Individualism/collectivism: Theory, method and application* (pp. 85–119). Sage.

Schwartz, S. H. (2006). A theory of cultural value orientations: Explication and applications. *Comparative Sociology, 5*(2–3), 137–182.

Schwartz, S. H. (2011). Studying values: Personal adventure, future directions. *Journal of Cross-Cultural Psychology, 42*(2), 307–319.

Senghor, L. S. (1964). *On African socialism* (M. Cook, Trans.). Pall Mall.

Senghor, L. S. (1994). Negritude: A humanism of the twentieth century. In P. Williams & L. Chrisman (Eds.), *Colonial discourse and postcolonial theory* (pp. 27–35). Columbia University Press.

Shadid, S. (2021). *Genealogies of philosophy: Michael O. Eze*. Blog of the American Philosophical Association. https://blog.apaonline.org/2021/01/08/genealogies-of-philosophy-m-onyebuchi-eze/. Consulted on 8 August 2022.

Smelser, N. J. (1992). Culture: Coherent or incoherent. In R. Munch & N. J. Smelser (Eds.), *Theory of culture*. University of California Press. http://ark.cdlib.org/ark:/13030/ft8q2nb667/

Smit, I., & Siegmund, W. (2014). *An engineer's Odyssey.* Siegmund audiovisuele produkties. https://www.youtube.com/watch?v=xbLjgm-9Pkw. Consulted 27 August 2023.

Smith, P. B., & Bond, M. H. (1999). *Social psychology across cultures* (2nd ed.). Allyn & Bacon.

Smith, P. B., Dugan, D., & Trompenaars, F. (1996). National culture and the values of organizational employees: A dimensional analysis across 43 nations. *Journal of Cross-Cultural Psychology, 27*(2), 231–264.

Smith, P. B., Trompenaars, F., & Dugan, S. (1995). The rotter locus of control scale in 43 countries: A test of cultural relativity. *International Journal of Psychology, 30*(3), 377–400.

Spivak, G. C. (1988). Can the subaltern speak? In C. Nelson & L. Grossberg (Eds.), *Marxism and the interpretation of culture* (pp. 271–313). Macmillan.

Stahl, G. K. (1998). *Internationaler Einsatz von Führungskräften*. München, Germany.

Taiye, S. (2005). *Bye-bye Babar*. http://thelip.robertsharp.co.uk/?p=76. Consulted on 5 January 2021.

Taras, V., Steel, P., & Kirkman, B. L. (2012). Improving national cultural indices using a longitudinal meta-analysis of Hofstede's dimensions. *Journal World Business, 47*(3), 329–341.

Taylor, I. (2018). *African politics: A very short introduction*. Oxford University Press.

Terray, E. (1986). Le climatiseur et la véranda. *Afrique plurielle, Afrique actuelle: Hommage a Georges Balandier*.
The Economist. (2015, January 22). *Foreign investment of Africa: A sub-Sahara scramble*. https://www.economist.com/business/2015/01/22/a-sub-saharan-scramble. Consulted on 5 October 2019.
Triandis, H. C. (1982). Review of culture's consequences: International differences in work-related values. *Human Organization, 41*(1), 86–90.
Trompenaars, F. (1993). *Riding the waves of culture*. Economist Books.
United Nations Development Programme. http://hdr.undp.org/en/countries/profiles/AGO. Consulted on 5 October 2019.
Vansina, J. (1990). *Path in the rainforest: Toward a history of political tradition in Equatorial Africa*. University of Wisconsin Press.
Vansina, J. (1992). A past for the future? *Dalhousie Review, 68*(1–2), 8–23.
Van Pinxteren, B. (2018). *African identities: A new perspective*. African Studies Centre.
Venkateswaran, R. T., & Ojha, A. K. (2019). Abandon Hofstede-based research? Not yet! A perspective from the philosophy of the social sciences. *Asia Pacific Business Review, 25*(3), 413–434. https://doi.org/10.1080/13602381.2019.1584487
Vonk, A. P. (2016). OD approaches in other cultures. *OD Practitioner, 48*(3), 13–21.
Vonk, A. P. (2017). Interactieve benaderingen langs de culturele meetlat. *M&O, 71*(1), 21–35.
Williamson, D. (2002). Forward from a critique of Hofstede's model of national culture. *Human Relations, 55*(11), 1373–1395.
Wind, Y., Douglas, P. S., & Perlmutter, V. H. (1973, April). Guidelines for developing international marketing strategies. *Journal of Marketing, 37*(2), 14–23.
Wiredu, K. (2008). Social philosophy in postcolonial Africa: Some preliminaries concerning communalism and communitarianism. *South African Journal of Philosophy, 27*(4), 332–339.
Wiredu, K. (2009). An oral philosophy of personhood: Comments on philosophy and orality. *Research in African Literatures, 40*(1), 8–18.
Wursten, H. (1997). Mental images the influence of culture on (economic) policy. In *Report of the international colloquium on regional governance and sustainable development*. United Nations Publication ST/ESA/PAD/SER. E, 46.
Wursten, H. (2019). *The 7 mental images of national culture: Leading and managing in a globalized world*. Helsinki.
Young, C. (1986). Africa's colonial legacy. In R. J. Berg & J. S. Whitaker (Eds.), *Strategies for African development* (pp. 25–51). University of California Press.
OECD. (2011). *Economic Diversification in Africa: a Review of selected Countries*. Paris: OECD Publishing.

Sharpley-Whiting, T. D. (2000). Femme negritude: Jane Nardal, La Depeche africaine, and the Francophone New Negro. In *Soul: Critical Journal of Black Politics & Culture, 2*(4), 8-17.

Nardal, P. & Sharpley-Whiting, T.D. (2014). *Beyond Negritude: Essays from Woman in the City.* State University of New York Press.

Blain, K.N. & Gill, T.M. (2019). *To turn the Whole World over: black women and internationalism.* University of Illinois.

Jackson, T (2013). Reconstructing the Indigenous in African Management Research. In Management International Review 53:13–38. DOI 10.1007/s11575-012-0161-0

Ahluwalia, P. (2001) *Politics and Post-colonial Theory: African Inflections.* London and New York, NY: Routledge

Noorderhaven, N.G. & Tidjani, B. (2001). Culture, Governance, and Economic Performance: An Explorative Study with a special focus on Africa. *International Journal of Cross Cultural Management 1*(1): 31-52.

Index

A. Vonk and V. F. Silva, *Cultural Confluence in Organizational Change*, Palgrave Studies in African Leadership,
https://doi.org/10.1007/978-3-031-45403-5

M

N

O

P

R

S

GPSR Compliance
The European Union's (EU) General Product Safety Regulation (GPSR) is a set of rules that requires consumer products to be safe and our obligations to ensure this.

If you have any concerns about our products, you can contact us on

ProductSafety@springernature.com

In case Publisher is established outside the EU, the EU authorized representative is:

Springer Nature Customer Service Center GmbH
Europaplatz 3
69115 Heidelberg, Germany

www.ingramcontent.com/pod-product-compliance
Ingram Content Group UK Ltd.
Pitfield, Milton Keynes, MK11 3LW, UK
UKHW020836290926
15470UKWH00004B/1381

* 9 7 8 3 0 3 1 4 5 4 0 2 8 *